Th
be
da

Glasgo
Librarie
names f

PRAISE FOR
THE REGENERATIVE LIFE AND CAROL SANFORD

"Carol is a rare educator. Utilizing regenerative thinking and approaches in our company, we began to produce significant cultural shifts across all levels and functional areas of our organization after only six months. Customers felt the difference, and associates found both their work and personal relationships becoming more purposeful, meaningful, and satisfying. The payoffs for the business were profound."

—Lara Lee, president, Orchard Supply Hardware,
a Lowe's company

"Carol has worked for many years with some of the most transformative companies of our time. Her work points to a way of being in the world that is simultaneously deeply pragmatic and an expression of transformative hope."

—Rebecca Henderson, John. H. Heinz endowed chair,
Harvard Business School

"Studying with Carol Sanford has blown my world, wide open. Carol is a contrarian in the best sense of the word, someone totally unseduced by popular opinion. As part of her Regenerative Life Community, I am continually surprised to find that what I've always taken for granted isn't actually set in stone, and that there is so much more potential in the world than I previously thought."

—Sheryl O'Loughlin, former CEO, REBBL, Clif Bar,
and founder and CEO, Plum Organics; executive director
of the Center for Entrepreneurial Studies, Stanford Graduate
School of Business

"*The Regenerative Life* frames a clear, authentic, and pragmatic approach for how we all have agency in creating a healthier society and our own inner transformation."

—Omar Brownson, cofounder and CEO of gthx and
leader in residence at NationBuilder

TESTIMONIALS FROM PARTICIPANTS IN THE REGENERATIVE LIFE ACTION RESEARCH PROJECT

"The regenerative life project helped me see who I'm being in my relationships and the communities that I'm part of through an entirely new lens."

—Jessica Handy, Education Program, Kiss the Ground, USA
Earth Tender Community

"The regenerative life project was transformational for me during the process of developing the concept of Rebl Mom. I highly encourage anyone to read it. It will change your life!"

—Moira Mills, founder, REBL Mom, USA
Regenerative Entrepreneur Community

"My engagement in the regenerative life project, and reading *The Regenerative Life* have been a transformative process into living from my essence and have provided me with a strong framework for intentionally designing my life and company to be more regenerative."

—Philippe Choinière, cofounder, ONEKA ELEMENTS, Canada
Regenerative Entrepreneur Community

"The regenerative life's frameworks and ideas were fundamental in helping me navigate the launch of an innovative and challenging program. They helped me to see past traditional barriers and constraints and work towards systems change, providing me with a language and set of tools to succeed."

—Maya Bahoshy, School of London, head of innovation, Great Britain
Regenerative Educator Community

"Carol Sanford's regenerative life frameworks gave me the courage to step outside the norm in ways that aligned with what I felt inspired to do but hadn't moved on because it countered most of the prevailing business advice."

—Ardell Broadbent, MA, game developer and mediator,
Politibanter, Canada
Regenerative Citizen Community

"Working in the regenerative life research project has been a powerful experience and definitely a disruptive one. It has completely changed some of my old behavioral patterns. I can now see clearly that we need to change our own patterns to have a regenerative effect in the system we are embedded in."

—Sidney Cano Melena, founder and CEO, DUIT, Mexico
Regenerative Entrepreneur Community

"The value of *The Regenerative Life* goes beyond my words. I would encourage anyone looking for ways to make a difference to read and try the ideas in this amazing book."

—Daimen Hardie, executive director, Community Forests International, Canada
Regenerative Earth Tender Community

"My work with Carol Sanford has finally given me the language and tools to start creating my own manual of good leadership—and not just a guide to leadership, but to life!"

—Frederik Christian Rasbech, CEO and storyteller, Twelves Pieces, Denmark
Regenerative Entrepreneur Community

"Involvement in the regenerative life project reinforced my role as a unique and creative individual."

—Bruno Dias, architect and designer, Portugal
Regenerative Designer Community

"Carol Sanford's *The Regenerative Life* makes explicit how each of us can do our part to heal the planet and make it feel whole again."

—Ian Johnson, senior director, Linnean Solutions, USA
Regenerative Earth Tender Community

"*The Regenerative Life* explores dynamic, regenerative frameworks that we can use to cultivate wholeness in ourselves and in the systems within which we are embedded."

—Mario M. Yanez, founding director, Inhabit Earth, USA
Regenerative Designer Community

"If the imperative to *be the change you want to see in the world* is important to you, then this is your book. The regenerative frameworks that Carol Sanford offers have challenged me to expand my own boundaries, reach toward higher levels of professional and personal potential, and develop the willful courage to lift my own offerings to new level."

—Geoff Stack, GIVE fellowship leader,
Business Volunteers Maryland, USA
Regenerative Educator Community

"The Regenerative Life makes Carol Sanford's concepts and practices available and accessible at last. My own growth and the regenerative effects on my community since I began this work have been remarkable."

—Trevanna Frost Grenfell, founder and director,
The Wildwood Path, USA
Regenerative Spirit Resource Community

"I highly recommend this book to anyone who takes seriously the need to transform our individual and collective thinking, doing, and being in the direction of regenerative cultures."

—Curtis Ogden, senior associate, Interaction Institute
for Social Change, USA
Regenerative Spirit Resource Community

"In these overstimulated and shrill times, we hunger for guides who carry simple messages that resonate. Many personal development authors aim for that but stop just below the surface. Carol digs deep. She works with no less an objective than to regenerate us and our world."

—Rachel Greenberger, cofounder and director,
Food Sol at Babson College, USA
Regenerative Educator Community

"Carol's teaching helps me put my meditation-oriented mind into action, finding ways to unleash potential in the critical players of this interconnected world so that we can achieve the systemic regeneration of life-giving energies."

—Yue "Max" Li, conservation research scientist, Arizona-Sonora
Desert Museum and University of Arizona School of Natural
Resources and the Environment, USA
Regenerative Earth Tender Community

"*The Regenerative Life* helped raise my awareness of how I was showing up as a designer."

—Edward McGraw, chief executive officer,
Ashley McGraw Architects, USA
Regenerative Designer Community

"In *The Regenerative Life*, Carol Sanford uses concise language and an ordered presentation to explore the application of regenerative principles and practices in personal and professional life. You will find this book illuminating and enlivening."

—Will Szal, Regen Network, USA
Regenerative Economic Shaper Community

"Carol Sanford's brilliance is the simplicity of the concepts she shares, which belies their immense power. They have helped me mentally unlock new ways to show up in life to greater effect and have become reminders I return to when I feel myself slipping back into more fearful modes of existence."

—Stephen Tracy, CEO, KEAP
Regenerative Entrepreneur Community

"The regenerative life project enabled me to understand the wholeness of my work and to feel the different places in me where the roles of entrepreneur, educator, spirit resource, and economic shaper live in action."

—Sarah Kerstin Gross, founder, C&K Community Kitchen, USA
Regenerative Entrepreneur Community

"This book is a must-read for anyone who considers themself to be a part of the simultaneously ancient and emerging paradigm of regeneration that the world so greatly needs in these times of climate change."

—Lily Hollister, storyteller, Kellogg Sister's Feed & Seed;
farmer, Lunasi Land Trust, USA
Regenerative Parent Community

"The regenerative life project enabled me to communicate the regenerative essence of my organization. I've also gotten more clarity on how the vision and the essence of the organization can resonate within the learning experiences we are offering."

—Emma Morris, Tuia Learning Environment, New Zealand
Regenerative Media Content Creator Community

"The regenerative journey I have been on over the last several years has actually changed my life. It is difficult to look back from this place and remember what it felt like to live without this deep, deeply human approach to work and life and everything in between."

—Frith Walker, manager Placemaking, Panuku
Development, New Zealand
Regenerative Citizen Community

"Working with the regenerative life frameworks has resulted in humbling recognition and honoring of a role that I didn't knowingly sign up for and have had difficulty accepting. This has allowed me to shift purpose and put my role into service."

—Ana Gabriela Robles, Desarrollo y ventas,
Latin America
Regenerative Spirit Resource Community

"The regenerative life project illuminated and helped me shift automatic patterns in a way that has massively increased my effectiveness in the world."

—Dan Palmer, *Making Permaculture Stronger*
podcast, New Zealand
Regenerative Media Content Creator Community

"Empowering! Discovering ourselves in one or more of the regenerative life roles affirms that by developing ourselves and our capability, whatever it is we already do can be done regeneratively."

—Kerstin Graebner, transition coach and cofounder,
Yoga Vana India, India
Regenerative Spirit Resource Community

"*The Regenerative Life* applies Carol's approach to the roles all of us play in both business and personal life. It will bring all sorts of new value."

—Sam Ford, Knight News Innovation fellow, Tow
Center for Digital Journalism at Columbia University, USA
Regenerative Citizen and Regenerative Media
Content Creator Communities

The Regenerative Life

Transform Any Organization,
Our Society, and Your Destiny

Carol Sanford

NICHOLAS BREALEY
PUBLISHING

BOSTON • LONDON

First published in 2020 by Nicholas Brealey Publishing
An imprint of John Murray Press

A Hachette UK company

25 24 23 22 21 20   1 2 3 4 5 6 7 8 9 10

A CIP catalogue record for this title is available from the British Library

Library of Congress Control Number:2019948850

ISBN 978-1-52930-821-1
US eBook ISBN 978-1-52931-193-8
UK eBook ISBN 978-1-52930-820-4

Printed and bound in the United States of America.

John Murray Press policy is to use papers that are natural, renewable and recyclable
products and made from wood grown in sustainable forests. The logging and
manufacturing processes are expected to conform to the environmental regulations of
the country of origin.

John Murray Press Ltd   Nicholas Brealey Publishing
Carmelite House   Hachette Book Group
50 Victoria Embankment   53 State Street
London EC4Y 0DZ   Boston, MA 02109, USA
Tel: 020 3122 6000   Tel: (617) 263 1834

www.nbuspublishing.com

To the perceptive and courageous participants in the regenerative life research project, who expressed their thinking and recounted their experiences with such verve! This would have been a much less lively book without your wholehearted participation.

Contents

Acknowledgments

I LOVE GENERATING NEW IDEAS in the creative process of writing a book. It clarifies and elevates my thinking, and the results seem to benefit others, as well.

For this book, Ben Haggard went beyond his *always* role of evolving my ideas into elegant offerings, evoking fitting images, and kicking out the superfluous. He suggested that I design an action research project to ensure that my thinking was grounded. He was a great partner in the articulation of each of the roles, and in particular, the regenerative Earth tender material is rich with his experience and characteristic articulation. He also skillfully ordered the entire book, making it an easy read from cover to cover.

Kit Brewer is a master copyeditor and has played this role for every book I have written. Her tenacity and rigor are helpful to Ben and me, and she contributes grace, rhythm, and a high level of aesthetic order to our work. This is what makes the reading so enjoyable.

And special thanks to Shannon Murphy, who advised us on the integrity of theme and continuity, which helped us discern the arc of the book, chapter by chapter and paragraph by paragraph.

To each of you I am eternally grateful. Without your engagement, my thinking would have a much rougher time finding its way into the world.

I also give thanks to the 92 adventurous people who participated in the action research project and the 50 who finished the race and submitted their stories. Your names appear in the book and your reflections are copiously quoted, so I will not list you here. *Take risk* is my favorite sign off, and you heard me and did it! You gave us a look at your development and evolution, bold and brave, which is something we rarely share so honestly. You are each a treasure, and I dedicate this book to you.

Foreword: From the Boardroom

I WORKED WITH CAROL SANFORD OVER a three-year period in the late 2000s, when I was cofounding CEO of Seventh Generation. We have both written about the impact her work had on the company, but I have not often discussed the effect it had on me personally. Carol engages everyone she touches within an organization systemically, based on the principles of regeneration, because she believes that to lift a business to the regenerative level you must develop all of its people. We spent hours and hours together—my team leaders and I put ourselves in her hands—and in the end her work had a transformational effect on me.

I believe that in order to transition to a fair, just, and sustainable world we must raise the consciousness of all of Earth's people. Some might argue that the other beings on the planet are already right where they need to be, creating the beautiful gardens we humans inhabit. In her long career, Carol has dedicated herself to evoking in us the level of awareness and capability needed to live in harmony with them.

The work I did with Carol helped me develop greater intention about who I wanted to become personally. I developed the capability to be more reflective and less reactive, and more aware of the unintended effects of my actions. Over time, I was able to become more honest, direct, and compassionate, and to create space for other people to blossom into their own possibilities and potential.

At Seventh Generation, we established a program of personal development and invited all of our employees into it. We also articulated the company's global imperative and developed a strategy to realize it. The growth this process fostered developed better friends, parents, and community members. While the business received and has delivered great benefit from this process, those who participated made many contributions outside of the workplace that have been just as extensive and valuable.

Throughout my life I have benefited from many teachers and mentors. It's rare that I'm not participating in some aspect of personal development. But, as I reflect on the work I did with Carol more than a decade ago, I am happy to share that it has *fundamentally* changed who I am and the role I play on the planet, and it is still giving back in the form of revitalizing contributions to social and environmental causes. The changes that Carol's developmental approach made in me have stood the test of time. I am deeply grateful for the gifts she shared with us and the impacts they have had. I have no doubt that as you dive into this life-changing book, you will also discover the power of her transformative thinking and that it will help you become who you seek to be.

Jeffrey Hollender, cofounder and CEO
American Sustainable Business Council

Foreword: From the News Desk

THERE IS NOTHING QUITE LIKE a rainstorm in the Midwest in the thick of summer. The heaviness of the air, hot and cold mixed together before the sounds of chaos arrive. In comes the rolling thunder; the lightning offers pyrotechnics before the main show. Finally, the downpour of rain, so heavy that sometimes as a girl, I'd watch in awe as the water flowed down from the roof of our house, catching air like sheets blowing in the wind.

The second act, one could argue, is always the aftermath. The city's grime washed away, the cool air offering sweet relief from the sweltering heat.

And then there is the carnage.

Worms, yes worms, are almost always the victims of Earth's wrath, spit out from the comfort of the soil onto the slippery cement. A heavy storm like this always pushes the limits of what soil can hold.

It is both a tragic and wondrous sight to see. I can't remember when I discovered it, but one day, like most kids, I took a stick and cut a worm in half. For a brief second I felt sorry for the earthworm as I watched it squirm. But then the miracle happened. The worm regenerated. A new body began to form as it made its way back to the grass and the dirt. Back to its home, to serve its purpose, which is to enrich the soil, the very element that spit it out.

Did you know that we also have the ability to regenerate? Not our bodies, of course, but our lives, *our purposes*. As you will learn from this book, through nine foundational roles we play in life, we too have the supreme power to renew ourselves after life's storms, to restore and build upon our work, for the greater good of society.

There is no one better to share this lesson than Carol Sanford. Carol is sharp, magnetic, an educator, and fiercely honest. She and I first met about a decade ago at a small business conference. I was a television journalist at the time and the emcee of the event, and Carol was the keynote speaker. I watched in awe as she brought her decades of experience as a thought leader and change agent in the business world to the mainstage. By the end of her presentation, the entire room was captivated by her wisdom. As Carol explains in *The Regenerative Life,* many of us carry out our roles in life unconsciously, unaware of the significance they play in society. This book reminds us of the enormous potential we have to shape society, and it gives us detailed resources for manifesting that power.

The Regenerative Life offers vitally important lessons, lessons we need to learn at this time in history, when democracy and civility are under attack. We are in the midst of a powerful storm, some of us pushed from our comfort zones and facing the journey of rebuilding ourselves so that we can be a part of the change we so desperately need.

As a broadcast journalist, my life's mission is to shed light in dark spaces. As you will learn from this book, my role as media content creator is to discern the truth, illuminate systemic effects, and make hope possible. I look forward to imparting the lessons learned from *The Regenerative Life* to grow and build on that mission, and I am confident you too will find new value in the roles you've chosen.

This book is for us.

Tonya Mosley, host of National Public Radio's *Here & Now*
Los Angeles, California, 2019

Introduction:
We Need a Better Theory

BELIEVE THAT MOST of us grow up with a pretty limited understanding of what it takes for an individual to create real change in the world. I base my belief on three basic narratives that I see repeated over and over. The first is the hero hypothesis: to save the day, a person needs to be superior, endowed with extraordinary skill and resources, staunchly committed to carrying the banner, fighting the good fight, and rousing the world out of its torpor, so that it lives up to the ideals they hold for it. The second basic narrative is that if we can't be a hero, then we need to find and follow a heroic leader, a charismatic someone who inspires us to pursue an ideal. The third basic narrative is that if we are as good as we can be—if we work long hours, recycle and compost, vote and donate, and especially if we are kind to dogs and children—then everything will be fine in the end.

Personally, I don't think we need more heroes or authorities. Those are storylines that reinforce the egoistic delusion that people are isolated actors who through sheer force of will can bend the world to their visions. By definition, only a few of us can be heroes, geniuses, or saints, which means that the rest of us are just clay waiting to be molded. What a terrible waste of human potential, spirit, intelligence, and creativity! It's interesting to note how easily we devalue ourselves and other people when we adopt a heroic mode.

I also see a built-in problem with the idea of doing good. There's a reason why people don't like do-gooders: do-gooders operate from the assumption that some people or some actions are by definition more virtuous than others. That is, goodness is a general standard or ideal, rather than something that arises from specific people within a specific set of circumstances. So it is *good* to reduce our consumption of resources, or go to church, or decry racism, because, "Well, it's self-evident isn't it?" Usually the do-gooder's definitions of virtue are memes or mores based on cultural or subcultural agreements (for example, political correctness or Christian piety) that are passed down generation to generation and therefore remain relatively unexamined. But these ideas of goodness are generic. They rob us of our responsibility to discover and choose ways of thinking and acting that might truly transform the specific situations we encounter in life.

For these reasons, I believe we need a better theory of change, one that goes beyond the heroic and do-good models and that taps into, develops, and releases the inherent potential of every human being to live in ways that make meaningful contributions to the world. Everything that follows in this book comes out of a theory of change that is

- *Developmental*—building systems-thinking skills and personal mastery
- *Essence sourced*—based on what makes every person or living thing specific and singular
- *Regenerative*—committed to realizing the evolutionary potential of life
- *Grounded*—based on the idea that we can transform our world by transforming the roles we play in our lives

It is, in other words, rooted in the evolutionary potential of human lives.

Dog Lawyer

Like most small children, I had a lot of will when I was very young. But unlike many, the difficulties of my circumstances only served to strengthen this will. I grew up in a broken and abusive family, in a broken place (the Texas panhandle), the granddaughter on my mother's side of a Native American man who had escaped the brokenness of early twentieth-century reservation life. My father was the Grand Dragon of the Texas KKK. When I was small, he locked me in a closet as a way to break my will. It didn't work. Instead, it reinforced my desire to stand up to him, to be a hero, and to break the corrosive influence of racism in my world.

There were many reasons for despair in my young life, but I was able again and again to allay my fears about the injustices of my world with fantasies of taking heroic actions to address them. One of my earliest ambitions was to be a dog lawyer! I thought it was outrageous that dogs were rounded up and put to sleep through no fault of their own and with no one to defend them. I was determined to become a heroic little-girl advocate for animal innocence.

By the time I was a college student, in the mid-1960s, I was putting my body on the line, marching in Berkeley to end racism and the Vietnam War. This earned me my first and only visit to jail and made me wonder where I would wind up in the long term. Was taking to the streets really making any kind of meaningful difference? I was beginning to have my doubts.

Not sure that I could be the hero I had imagined myself to be, I looked for heroes to support—political candidates who were advocating radical change to the system and intellectual leaders who were pointing to different ways to live in society. For a short while, Joseph Campbell reignited my excitement about the hero's journey, and I vowed once again to dedicate myself to changing the world. At the time, I was not yet mature enough to fully grasp two things Campbell was teaching us. First, the mythic hero's journey is always in service to and supported by a community. Second, it is intended to achieve some larger beneficial effect; the hero returns with a treasure that will alter the community's role within its world. Ultimately there is no independent heroic ego, only the collective work of sustaining and evolving life by reshaping the relationships between the community and its larger context.

A few years later, I began to study with inventor and philosopher

Arthur Young, founder of the Institute for the Study of Consciousness in Berkeley. Young had, among other things, invented the first long-distance helicopter. But his real interest was the thinking process that allowed people to accomplish these kinds of breakthroughs. He advocated for a process philosophy, one that directed its attention to inner development rather than outward advocacy and action.

These themes continued to work on me. Where was that heroic vision of my childhood? Could I ever become a hero? If not, then who was I? Was life really worth living? Pressed to make meaning of my life, yet seemingly denied outlets for these energies, I threw myself into a kind of compromise—be a good citizen. I volunteered with the League of Women Voters, struggled to be a good mother, separated my recyclable garbage. This way of life came nowhere close to satisfying my powerful inner promptings, and I began to slip into despair. What I failed to realize was that I didn't have an adequate theory of change. I believed that change came only from heroes and saints acting on behalf of all the small people around them.

Developing People

Happily, it was at this moment that I met a network of change designers based in Carmel, California. This group had discovered that profound change could happen through the almost invisible work of *developing the capacity of ordinary people to see things differently*. My advocacy work had been based on the assumption that I needed to force others to see things the way I saw them. This work, by contrast, acknowledged that every person had the inherent possibility to see beyond the immediate pressures, constraints, and opportunities of daily existence to the patterns that lay behind them. In other words, people can learn to see essence and potential and work together creatively to manifest them.

What a liberating thought! Transformation of the world lies hidden within the undeveloped capacity of every person. All that's needed are opportunities for us to develop ourselves, for us to learn to see things as they actually work so that change can flow from how we carry out our lives. This was my first intuition of the non-heroic journey. I didn't need to become something I wasn't in order to cause (or force) other people to change. I needed to join with them, to care about the things they cared about, in order to help them create the change they were already seeking.

I understood this idea almost the minute I joined the Carmel group, and soon after I had my first opportunity to witness its real power in action. I joined a business team that was working with engineers at DuPont who were trying to figure out better ways to work with titanium dioxide. This was an expensive material to produce, in both ecological and economic terms. With the gentlest of means—dialogue, probing questions, and systemic frameworks that encouraged them to learn how to manage their own thinking processes—we were able to help this group of engineers gain profound insight into the properties of the material, insights that changed forever the way it was produced. Within a few months, we were able to end years of mountain and stream destruction in Australia, where titanium was mined.

The changes we helped create at DuPont were profound, even revolutionary. They led to a completely new and proprietary process that allowed the company to extract high-grade titanium from small quantities of low-grade ore. But the methods we used to achieve this breakthrough were non-heroic. We were simply helping people do their jobs better by educating their thinking. These were ordinary, well-meaning individuals, attempting to do their best with the tasks in front of them. By focusing on the ways they thought about how to carry out these tasks, we were able to help them transform an entire industry. They became change agents from *within* the roles they had chosen to play in their companies and communities.

This point may seem so obvious that we can easily miss its significance. For me, the evolution of society is a collective activity. It doesn't come from the heroic actions of one political or military genius or the entrepreneurial insights of a great business leader, although these make great subjects for the stories we tell. Rather, it comes from *waking up and developing millions of people to the systemic benefits that can flow from thinking better about how they play their chosen daily roles in society.* We make a better world by teaching ordinary people practices for shifting their thinking processes and enabling themselves to show up as parents, employees, citizens, and neighbors in completely new ways.

Of course, this shift in mind is exactly what's needed to create successful families, businesses, civic organizations, and even governments. It's no accident that I spent many years working in business systems. I recognized early on that they offered excellent platforms for doing this transformational work. But really, my purpose all along was to help individuals develop greater consciousness and agency with regard to their own thinking, in order to allow far more beneficial actions to flow from it. For this reason, my earlier books focused almost entirely on businesses. This book looks at the other side of the same coin: what each of us can do in our own lives, through the many roles that we play at home, at work, and in the world. It's a personal book, and many of its stories are personal. But it's also a book about the fundamentals that are needed to create healthy economies and societies.

Personal Transformation at DuPont

One of the people who worked on DuPont's titanium project was a young engineer named Jack Michelson. His team was responsible for transforming titanium ore into titanium dioxide at the company's plant in DeLisle, Mississippi. Jack had come to DuPont straight out of graduate school and had a gift for motivating people. He was enthusiastic and energetic, and like a good general, he could transmit this enthusiasm to others.

But when I met him, Jack was fiercely divided within himself. As a conscientious person, he wanted to do good in the world. He dedicated himself to environmental causes in his private life and to excellence at work, but he experienced these two sides of his life as conflicting with each other. So when we began to discover ways to use his work life to transform the environmental impacts of his industry, he was on fire and ready to rouse the troops and lead the charge.

Of course, this was a manifestation of his old heroic mode. It didn't take us long to help him realize that becoming an ecological advocate inside the company wasn't the point either, because this still meant promoting his own point of view rather than tapping into what was meaningful for his colleagues. He could see that the power of what we were doing lay in helping everyone use their own intelligence and con-scientiousness to contribute to a better world. This insight completely transformed the way he worked as a manager, from motivational hero to resource.

The proprietary changes underway in DuPont's titanium refinement process required the radical redesign of the DeLisle plant in a very short time. Jack discovered that it wasn't necessary or appropriate to be the hero supplying the enthusiasm that would motivate his team. Instead, we needed to help them develop new thinking capabilities that would enable them to recognize the significance of what they were doing—and therefore discover how to work differently. When they could see for them-selves the importance of these changes for their industry, they were able to supply their own will and enthusiasm. Jack had learned the difference between exhorting people and developing them—between being a white knight riding to the rescue and a co-learner holding the container within which everyone could grow.

Being Non-Heroic

I introduce the idea of the non-heroic journey as an antidote to heroic psy-chology. Heroism is sometimes necessary in emergencies, but it is always counterproductive to making enduring change. The Chinese philosopher Lao Tzu wrote, "Water is fluid, soft, and yielding. But water will wear away rock, which is rigid and cannot yield. As a rule, whatever is fluid, soft, and yielding will overcome whatever is rigid and hard.... This is another paradox: what is soft is strong."[1]

The non-heroic path is a journey. It comes from learning how to live our lives and play our roles in ways that are designed to create change. It doesn't get turned on with a surge of adrenaline and turned off again with a burst of over-the-top action. It is slow, steady, cumulative, and power-ful, like water shaping rock. It depends on coming to know ourselves, understanding how our minds work, and learning to shape and direct creative energies.

Non-heroism happens in everyday life, with all of the imperfec-tions and incompleteness that are simply part of being human. You don't need to sacrifice the things you love or give up the ordinary joys of hav-ing a job, a family, and neighbors. Non-heroic undertakings need not be grandiose to make a profound difference. What they require is an ability to see how the work we are doing—*any* work we are doing—can play a critical role within society. Our effects can be direct, through the influence we have on social institutions, or indirect, by preparing oth-ers (for example, our children) to play their roles. When we understand our role, it becomes possible to work at the level of home, classroom, entrepreneurial business, or neighborhood to create the better society for which we all long.

Is the Regenerative Life for You?

When we ask children what they want to be when they grow up, none of them choose something small. They all want something meaningful or that serves a deep purpose. When we're young, we have aspirational visions that are BIG, and we are sure that when we're adults, we'll finally have the wherewithal to enact them. Much of children's play is connected to big visions.

But these visions get lost along the way as we grow up. They feel too challenging. Why? Why is it that once we've gotten established in the world, we let go of them? For many young professionals, the problem isn't so much a loss of dreams and aspirations. Rather, it's a sense of despair, a belief that the world has been running backward for so long that there's no place for them to pursue their dreams. If you are struggling with how to make real meaning from your life and work, this book is intended to for you.

Work is where we put our life energy, and we tend to define our work in terms of career. Yet this can be too narrow a way to frame our sense of what work is. We have the option instead to think of ourselves as pursuing particular roles in society, roles that at their core are meant to improve and transform the communities and industries we are part of. This transformational work is what lies behind those childhood aspirations to make meaningful contributions. Viewed from this perspective, our work isn't something we do to earn a livelihood while we make social contributions as volunteers on the side. Our work is directly connected to the contributions we aim to make. But this requires us to think deeply about what work is, what we bring to it, and how we do it.

The current generation has grown up with a worldview that understands certain core truths: we humans have to change the way we live on the planet and become participants in living systems, relationships are at least as important to a good life as material success, and work is a place where we can contribute to a better world. For this generation, the political and economic struggles that preoccupy their elders and absorb so much media attention are a sideshow that will be swept away by their emerging demographic power. They know that they will soon be living in a very different world and culture because they are already creating it. In other words, they are forming a collective image of what society's future purpose and form should be. This book is intended as a response to them. It lays out the key roles from which it will be possible to regenerate society.

How to Read *The Regenerative Life*

Before we continue, let's take a few moments to consider how best to process the material that appears in this book.

Use the Frameworks

Every chapter is organized around a living-systems framework that is derived from close observation of how life works. I strongly encourage the adoption of these frameworks because they

1. enable us to better understand and work with complex phenomena, and
2. allow us to manage the complexity of our own minds.

I mentioned earlier that a shift of mind is a powerful way to work on changing the world. Frameworks are the key to this shift.

I am not referring here to mental models, which are the rigid codes that govern our behavior and problem solving. The manners we learn from our parents, for example, represent an accepted code or pattern of conduct within particular contexts, such as how to behave at the dinner table. The power of mental models is that they readily become automatic and unconscious—they program us. But this is also their downside. A mental model inserts itself into our mental processes, presenting itself as our only natural or available option for dealing with a given situation. For this reason, we carry out automatic patterns of behavior—even when they are inappropriate or in violation of our values—without noticing that we're doing so.

Frameworks have precisely the opposite purpose. Instead of programming us, they break our programming. They encourage consciousness, systemic thought, and careful consideration of what is appropriate in a specific situation. Of course, they can only serve this purpose if we engage them in a conscious way. It can be all too easy to convert a living framework into a machine-like mental model.

I remember the moment when I finally realized how powerful a framework could be in my life. As a young woman, I never really thought of myself as a writer. I could generate a profusion of good ideas, but the discipline of organizing them so that other people could follow them was not, to put it mildly, my strong suit. In my early forties, I submitted a chapter for a book titled *Learning Organizations*, in which I presented a characteristically contrarian point of view.[2] The editor came back to me and explained that while she was enthusiastic about the ideas in the article, she was deeply dismayed that she could not understand how they hung together. I went back to look at what I'd written, and I could see the underlying structure—or framework—it contained. However, I could also see that I had not made this framework explicit for my readers. Once I named it and clearly described it, the article made more sense. I vowed to never write anything in the future without first articulating, at least to myself, the framework that supplied its coherence.

For me, frameworks provide a structure that can help me manage all of the different dimensions and complexities of whatever I'm working on. Instead of losing myself in the details, I'm able to hold a dynamic image in my mind of the relationships among different, sometimes competing, ideas. This allows me to work with the details without ever losing my place in the big picture. It is to share these benefits that I offer the frameworks in this book. There are lots of interesting ideas and details to get lost in, but there is always an organizing structure to help you place them in context.

In particular, I've used a familiar framework to organize the core content of this book—the enneagram. I mention this because the enneagram has very much entered popular culture, and in the process it has been downgraded to a typology, which is a mental model. Understood as a framework, the enneagram helps reveal the patterns of relationship and energy hidden within the dynamics of transformation. In this case, I'm using it to help us see how we can work together to transform society.

The conclusion of *The Regenerative Life* is dedicated to an in-depth look at how the enneagram framework applies to this important work.

Take It Personally

Another suggestion for processing material in this book is to make it your own at the personal level. If we are to live regenerative lives—if we are to break old, unconscious patterns of belief and come at things in new, more conscious ways—then we must allow regenerative ideas and ways of applying them to enter and change us. Put in a slightly different way, we need to avoid approaching the material presented here as knowledge, as an improved mental model. Instead, we need to approach it as a question, a provocation, a challenge. *The Regenerative Life* won't be helpful if it's received as my ideas. It will only become helpful when it has been tested by your own lived experience.

For this reason, I suggest that you start a journal to record your impressions and experiences in parallel to your reading. Don't make notes about what I've written or your thoughts about it. Instead, make notes about what happened when you applied what you read to something meaningful in your life. What changed? What are you seeing differently? What could happen next to extend this learning?

You will notice that in many places I've illustrated my points with personal examples from my own life. I've also included stories from people who applied these concepts in their lives and what happened to them as a result. I'm hoping that by the time you reach the end, you'll be able to supply examples from your life as well!

Take It to Work

Once we've begun to take these ideas personally and have committed in an ongoing way to disrupting our unconscious patterns, we're ready to apply what we've learned in all of our endeavors. Most of us begin by developing our roles within family and community, but it is important to bring our inner changes into the workplace as well. Work is where we invest a large part of our time, energy, and creativity. Questions to ask ourselves in this context are

- "How do I shake loose of my job description, a mental model imposed and maintained by others with my assent?" and
- "Instead, how do I learn to see myself playing a living, evolving role that will make my company or organization more successful at fulfilling its purpose?"

Reflecting on these questions can help us unleash our creative energies and put them to use toward a meaningful purpose. But they become even more relevant for those of us who are in the role of managers or leaders. From the perspective of a regenerative life, the work of a manager is not to tell other people what to do, but to help them develop and utilize their own intelligence and energy in service to the larger goals and missions of the organization.

CHAPTER ONE

Beyond the Heroic

A S I PROPOSED in the introduction, the heroic hypothesis assumes that systemic change requires visionary leaders who expend huge amounts of energy and will in order to make a difference in the world. The heroic path sees change as a matter of scale: if it isn't big, then it's not making a difference. In other words, change is quantitative and outwardly focused. But what if the most powerful change processes depend on qualitative rather than quantitative shifts? What if who we're becoming has more influence than how much stuff we're doing?

The non-heroic path seeks a way to create profound and enduring change, not through large-scale movements or fighting the good fight, but by enabling people to transform themselves. When people learn how to evolve their own thinking—their beliefs, perspectives, aspirations, and thought patterns—they become change catalysts in all parts of their lives and with everyone they touch. Social movements are built on the power of certain compelling ideas. But regenerative change is built on the power of taking conscious charge of our thinking processes and helping others to do the same.

When we choose this path, we function like a helpful virus, one that fosters the vitality and immune system of the host (for example, by supporting healthy intestinal bacteria) while at the same time protecting against harmful viruses. By helping its host to thrive, a helpful virus is able to spread as a beneficial symbiont.

Medical science is becoming more and more appreciative of the internal populations of bacterial and viral species in the human body, the cooperation among them, and their role in the maintenance of human well-being. This is an ecosystem perspective that brings new sophistication to our overall understanding of health.

Compare this to the practice of developing drugs to fight unfriendly viruses. When we use an antiviral drug, we trigger a biochemical arms race, with nasty viruses racing to out-survive the latest pharmaceutical invention. In contrast, nurturing a community of helpful viruses builds the systemic ability of host organisms as a whole to manage attacks.

This example is intended to illustrate a critical shift in our approach to social change. Current political and social discourse has become polarized, at times to such an extent that we are immobilized, unable as a society to take necessary or beneficial actions even in dire emergencies. As long as we continue to dig our feet in, holding strongly to our own beliefs or political positions, we reinforce this situation of social stasis. Regardless of where we are on the political spectrum—left, right, center, or none of the above—as long as we make ourselves right and the others wrong, we have no choice but to battle it out at the ballot box, through demonstrations, or in the media. We are trying to function like an antiviral drug, while our opponents are figuring out ways to make end runs around us. What a huge expenditure of energy just to make incremental and often temporary changes!

Levels of Perspective

The irony is that when we are in this situation, we become victims of our own lack of perspective. We can see the merits of our own point of view, but we struggle to understand and accept the merits of the opposition's. This metaphor of point of view is apt: our perspective has collapsed into a single point.

In the late 1800s, a British philosopher named Edwin Abbott wrote a witty little book, *Flatland*, to illustrate this problem.[1] In it, the residents of a two-dimensional world struggle to imagine a world of three dimensions. Their two-dimensional perspective means that they can see a sphere only as a circle. When they visit a one-dimensional world, the problem gets even worse. Residents of a one-dimensional world see everything as points.

Abbot vividly illustrates the influence of our perspective and thinking patterns on how we perceive reality. More important, he shows that there are different levels of perspective. When we collapse our vision, we lose our ability to see the full range of possibilities that lie hidden in plain view. To access these possibilities, we only need to recover our ability to explore multiple points of view from a level of perspective that sees their potential relatedness.

The problem is that we tend to become attached to the things we really believe in. For example, we may passionately reject the exploitation of people and natural systems. But as soon as we set ourselves up as opponents to those we see as exploiters, we end up in heroic battles over everything from Supreme Court nominations to fishing practices. We still find ourselves trying to stop the nasty viruses instead of introducing beneficial viruses to create an environment of balance and healthy function.

Understanding the Idea of Levels

So what exactly do I mean by *levels*? Before I talk about them in the context of perspective, here's an example from sports.

Parents often encourage their children to play a sport, such as soccer, as a way to gain basic functional skills. As children play, they develop their coordination, learn teamwork, and grow the ability to handle setbacks. At this stage in their lives, they are in the game for what it can give to them rather than what they can give to it.

By the time they're in high school, on a school team competing in intramural games, they have progressed to dedicating themselves to the sport. Teenage athletes focus on refining their performance and eliminating weaknesses or bad habits; they play for the team, as well as for themselves. They are at a different stage of development, playing at a completely different level than young children.

Players at the college level have usually been recruited for their soccer skills. At this level, they are expected to work on improving themselves—the discipline, intelligence, and integrity with which they play—as well as to work on their skills. With the eye of the public on them, they understand that their performance is a reflection of the character of the team and possibly of the college as a whole.

At the professional level, if soccer players are to achieve the apex of their potential, they must dedicate themselves not only to their own development, but also to expressing the essence of their teams and of the game itself. When professional players join a great team, they are trained in its distinctive game or approach. They also learn strategy, reading the games of other teams in order to figure out how to use their own strategizing to prevail in competition. For a really great team, all this work plays out on a world stage, where the game becomes a visible metaphor for courage, grace, honor, and beauty—inspiring its fans and thereby securing the future of the sport.

This example of the development of soccer players suggests what I mean by levels. At each stage of their development, players shift to a new level of performance, as well as a new scope with regard to what they take into consideration. These changes in level correlate to a corresponding growth in maturity. A simple glance at the headlines will show that there are plenty of professional athletes who behave badly, but this can be understood as a failure to mature fully through all of the levels and take on the responsibilities that come with them.

Additionally, the soccer example also suggests that higher levels of engagement, corresponding to more advanced stages of development, don't replace the need for the lower levels. Even as a professional player, it's necessary to maintain and evolve basic skills and coordination. Ideally, the different levels work together and complement one another, so long as they are informed by the highest level the athlete has attained.

Levels of Paradigm

My soccer example is a special case of a more general framework that I call "Levels of Paradigm." Paradigms provide context for our lives and work; they determine our perspectives and shape the choices we make and the actions we take. They are often unconscious, which means that it rarely occurs to us to examine them. It's even rarer to recognize that our paradigms operate at different levels and that these levels have very different implications in terms of the quality of the effects that flow from our choices and actions. (Note that the following framework is read from bottom to top—from lower to higher level.)

Regenerate Life
Do Good
Arrest Disorder
Value Return

In the case of a soccer player, we can see that an upward shift in level enables a greatly expanded scope for development, accomplishment, and impact. Children play soccer for the value it generates in terms of strength or controlled reflexes. Teenagers play it as an arena to hone their skills and correct the flaws in their performance. College athletes play it to express their potential and gain accolades. Professionals on teams that achieve greatness evolve the game and encourage millions of fans to pursue aspirational lives.

The foundational paradigm in this framework is *Value Return*. Within this paradigm, we expect that when we invest money, time, or effort into something, it will generate a useful return. We seek out and adopt patterns that have been proven to deliver similar results in the past. For example, teachers use tried-and-true pedagogical methods to ensure that students will learn what is required of them. Investors follow proven models for generating financial returns. Engineers apply best practices to designing highways, airplanes, or software. The idea is to reliably reproduce a pattern of behavior or action in order to achieve predictable results.

The next paradigm, *Arrest Disorder*, shifts us to managing entropy in a continuously changing world. It's not enough to focus on a specific action, assuming that if we do it well, we'll always achieve the same result, because the context within which the action is occurring is changing. For example, a soccer player needs to know not only how to kick the ball down the field, but also how to do so in relationship to all of the other players who are in motion and pursuing their own strategies. In the same way, a software or computer engineer is designing within a field that is evolving from one day to the next.

When we work from this level of paradigm, we are seeking ways to manage both our own actions and the context within which they occur, usually by addressing gaps and problems that are showing up. For example, we might become more strategic about how our actions fit with what's happening in the marketplace (coming up with a smartphone app that fills a need no one else seems to see, let's say). Or we might choose to improve flawed practices within a profession or an industry that consistently lead to waste or inferior results. However we approach it, we need to stay abreast of changes happening in our field and in the world, taking them into account in our decisions and seeking to ensure that the end results are beneficial to those who will be impacted.

When we begin to work within the *Do Good Paradigm*, we operate from a faith in the potential of things and people to improve and make more meaningful contributions to the world. This allows us to look at more than the immediate consequences of our actions. We're motivated by a desire to manifest the potential we can see, to make the world a better place. Not only do we need to pay attention to our actions and their context, but also we need to build our own character, so that we're able to be consistent and honorable with regard to these motivations.

Adopting this level of paradigm will have the effect of stretching us, enlarging our compassion and touching us personally. For example, we might join the board of a nonprofit agency that's seeking to make life better for children, or we might volunteer to mentor children directly. The work is no longer at arm's length. It requires giving ourselves fully to something other than ourselves and absorbing the lessons that will inevitably arise from the uncertainty inherent in working with real, living beings facing real-life challenges.

The *Regenerate Life Paradigm* focuses on how to build the capacity in people and other living systems to be self-determining in the world. At this level, we make a profound shift in perspective. We commit to seeking what's essential in each person and every sort of thing that is the subject of our work. We become radically particular. We are no longer willing to pigeonhole people, places, groups, or materials because we see each as unique. When we make this shift, we're able to enter into deeply respectful relationships, where the full expression of the unique potentials of others is our primary objective.

As the highest level of paradigm in our framework, *regenerate life* incorporates and transforms how we work on all of the others. We're still willing to *do good*, but not in a generic or abstract way. The good we seek starts from an essence that wants to be expressed. We may still wish to reduce waste and dysfunction by *arresting disorder* in a system, but we never allow this to distract us from the overall creative purpose we're pursuing. And we certainly need to achieve a *value return* from our efforts if we're to be able to continue them, but value return includes the fulfillment that arises from realizing the potential of someone or something other than ourselves.

As a general rule, these different levels correspond to different phases of our development. We can see this reflected in the soccer player example earlier, where the players advance from child to adult by steadily enlarging and deepening the scope of their conscious awareness. But these phases often reassert themselves when we take on a significantly new endeavor or role in our lives. I know in my own life, whenever I push myself to take on something new (for example, teaching myself to be a writer!), I feel like a child again, awkward and struggling to make things work (value return). But little by little I develop enough basic competence to start working on self-improvement (arresting disorder), aspiring to excellence (doing good), and ultimately contributing to a better world (regenerating life).

Of course, it takes consciousness and will to move ourselves through all four of these developmental phases or levels. Because our modern world and culture place such emphasis on analytical dissection, problem solving, individualism, and compartmentalization, we have to exert extraordinary effort to move ourselves up to paradigms of dynamism and development. The first step is to become aware that the levels exist and that it is possible to make choices with regard to them.

Paradigms in Action

If our intention is to live a regenerative life, then we need to learn to recognize which paradigm we're currently working from and which paradigms are driving the decisions and actions of the people around us. This ability enables us to become more conscious of our thinking and behavioral patterns, setting the stage for our own development while growing our capacity to help others in their development.

To accomplish this, we bring dimensionality to each of the paradigms, showing *how* it shapes the way we think and act. The framework for this work is the four-pointed tetrad, which describes the particular forces at work within each paradigm. Generically, these forces are described as the *ground* on which our thinking is based, the *goal* that it is directed toward, the *instruments* we characteristically use to reach the goal, and the *direction* that guides the overarching way we stay on track. Let's look at each paradigm in action, with the aid of the tetrad.

Value Return Paradigm

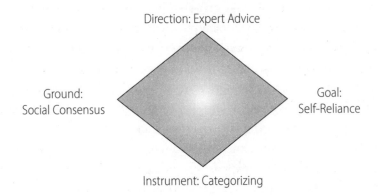

Direction: Expert Advice

Ground:
Social Consensus

Goal:
Self-Reliance

Instrument: Categorizing

When we are driven by value return, the goal is to make choices that either preserve or strengthen our position in relationship to the world around us. "Look out for number one!" as people commonly put it. (Another way this goal gets expressed is through the metaphor of "maintaining our boundaries.") Obviously, there are many situations that have the potential to drain our energy and resources if we don't maintain some awareness of what's healthy and appropriate for us. On the other hand, this attitude can become defensive, cutting us off from the world.

The Value Return Paradigm grounds itself in the certainty that comes from social consensus. Many of our basic social agreements have developed slowly and were handed down for generations. They provide a familiar territory within which to operate. By basing our decisions and actions on this social consensus, we avoid the risks and possible ostracism that come from striking out on an untried path.

At this level of paradigm, we turn to expert advice to help us make the right choice or head in the right direction. Recognizing that we have limited time to do research, that we have inadequate skills, and/or that we have a low tolerance for risk, we look for someone who is more knowledgeable or experienced to tell us what we should do.

When taking action in accordance with this paradigm, we work from well-defined ground rules, usually based on generally agreed upon criteria for what works best. These ground rules allow us to move quickly and confidently, sorting and categorizing our options, and making choices that are consistent with proven practices. The downside, of course, is that a life played by the rules, whether our own or someone else's, limits our opportunities for creativity and self-discovery.

The Value Return Paradigm is useful in situations where we feel we need to limit the complexity or hazard that we are managing, such as undergoing training in return for learning a new skill or opening a savings account as a safe way to generate a little income. However, problems arise when we keep using value return to manage every aspect of our lives. It isolates us from the dynamism and complexity of real human relationships and a living, changing world.

Arrest Disorder Paradigm

Direction: Living Up to Standards

Ground: Prioritizing Critical Issues

Goal: Awakening Stewardship

Instrument: Problem Solving to Reduce Degradation

Behind the Arrest Disorder Paradigm is an implicit assumption that there is in any situation a proper order for things, a standard below which conditions should never drop. When we find ourselves confronted with conditions that do not meet our standards (for example, the lake is polluted, the business is losing money, or income inequality is growing), we go into action to do something about it. In other words, when we operate from an arrest disorder perspective, our goal is to get people to wake up and take responsibility for the integrity of social and ecological systems. We seek to foster a culture of stewardship or guardianship among our colleagues, fellow citizens, or relevant institutions.

Arresting disorder is grounded in a strong sense of the problems that need to be addressed. Indeed, if we are working from this paradigm, it's important to start from real clarity about which are the most critical problems and issues and how to prioritize them if we are to get things back on track. As the saying goes, "Knowing where to start is half the battle." The classic instruments for working at this level are the various tools that allow us to break problems into parts so that they can be understood and addressed. This allows us to zero in on the options and alternatives that are most likely to resolve issues in ways that meet our standards.

The Arrest Disorder Paradigm is useful for helping individuals, communities, and organizations keep from losing ground with regard to potentially destructive phenomena. It allows us to feel a sense of accomplishment when in some way we've helped things work better. It's no accident that this paradigm and the problem-solving approaches it fosters are enormously popular in our culture. Indeed we promote them, teach them, and celebrate the accomplishments of people who have successfully applied them to address the innumerable issues confronting us. However, arresting disorder also severely limits our attention, creativity, and actions to fixing problems that have their origins in the past. Given the nature of human ingenuity, there are much larger, future-directed arenas that we could choose to play in—which leads us to the next level of paradigm.

Do Good Paradigm

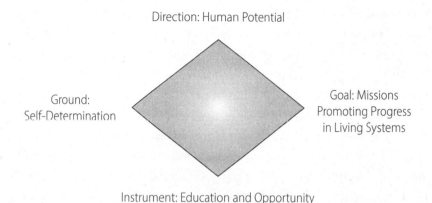

Direction: Human Potential

Ground:
Self-Determination

Goal: Missions
Promoting Progress
in Living Systems

Instrument: Education and Opportunity

The goal for work at the Do Good Paradigm level is to awaken an activated sense of desire and mission to promote progress for human beings and all other natural systems. This is different from the stewardship or guardianship we find at the Arrest Disorder level, which is mostly about keeping things as they are or restoring them to what they once were. Progress, on the other hand, is focused on what things could become if they were given the opportunity.

This sense of mission and agency is grounded in the belief that we can take charge of our own destinies and dedicate ourselves to making the world a better place, not limiting ourselves to doing damage control with regard to the mistakes of the past. At this level, we experience people as having free will. We become more than the products of our genetics, upbringing, class, or training. We are the protagonists in our own lives.

The development of this kind of agency is the primary focus of the human potential movement, whose theories and practices provide articulation and orientation for the overall thrust of doing good. People who set out to realize their potential do so from an experience of self-direction. They have rejected the boxes that society or parents placed them in and discovered depths and capacities within themselves that long to be expressed. Because they have had a direct, personal experience of this awakening, they have an unshakeable faith that others can have it too.

This faith can lead to a kind of missionary zeal, with its attendant pitfalls. But at its best, the Do Good Paradigm gets expressed through the instrument of education, calling forth the potential in others by engaging them in a process of self-discovery. At its worst, it can become coercive, with practitioners attempting to convert their listeners by convincing, persuading, influencing, or even conquering them for their own good. This is one of the reasons that do-gooders can become annoying or even alienating.

The usefulness of the Do Good Paradigm arises from the way it allows us to see more possibility in the world for ourselves and others. This comes in part from the transition we make when we move from value return and arresting disorder to doing good. Often described metaphorically as *waking ourselves up*, it gives us new access to our agency, the fact that we are responsible for how we experience life, and the wealth of meaning to be found in the world outside ourselves.[2]

But there is also a hazard in awakening. At the level of doing good, it can be experienced as conversion, and this can lead to proselytizing. If we try to impose our experience on others as gospel—"I found religion [or permaculture or holocracy or fill-in-the-blank], and I've just *got* to share it with you"—then we foreclose on their authentic discovery processes. This can lead to a fixed belief in our own certainty, setting the stage for intolerance or even cultishness, and shutting down our own ongoing learning.

Regenerate Life Paradigm

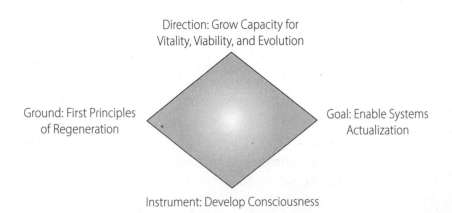

Direction: Grow Capacity for
Vitality, Viability, and Evolution

Ground: First Principles
of Regeneration

Goal: Enable Systems
Actualization

Instrument: Develop Consciousness

The goal for work at the Regenerate Life Paradigm level is to enable living systems actualization. Too often, people conceive of systems as aggregations of parts, but this misses the point. We actually experience an entity as a living system when we perceive it as a singular whole. At first glance, this may seem a bit abstract or difficult, but it becomes fairly obvious when we use a child as an example. Individual children are something more than the sum of their various parts. It is possible to think of them each as a bag of bones, guts, and brain, but doing so clearly violates our sense of the essential meanings of their human lives.

Once we have this perception, we are able to engage with a system as a coherent whole, with its own tendency toward aliveness and its own need to secure a place in the world by making beneficial contributions. To enable living systems actualization means to perceive phenomena in terms of their wholeness and dynamic aliveness rather than their thingness, and to take actions and make choices in support of the full expression of this aliveness.

Returning to the example of little children, if we have some responsibility for their well-being, then we wish them to become self-determining and to actualize themselves as unique individuals. This has to do with enabling them to express their creativity, but it also means helping them find ways to make meaningful contributions to the world. Of course, this is true not just for individual people but for all living systems, including soil, bodies, families, communities, businesses, gardens, forests, and watersheds, all the way up to Earth as a whole and beyond.

At the Regenerate Life level, our focus is on what makes things alive. This requires anchoring our work in the first principles of living systems, the ground from which it becomes possible to understand them. When we have a clear sense of these first principles, we're quickly able to assess whether or not the work we're doing is therefore regenerative.

The overall direction toward which work at this level is oriented is to grow capacity for vitality, viability, and evolution. This implies that regenerative work respects the autonomy and self-determination of living systems and is committed to helping them become increasingly good at accomplishing their own actualization. If this is not our direction, we may imagine a heroic role for ourselves, in which we tell other living beings who they are, what they should become, and how they should behave. But this robs them of their agency, their potential for development, and their ability to make their own unique contributions to the world based on their own creative discoveries.

For this reason, the Regenerate Life Paradigm depends on our ability to restrain our heroic impulses. The key to rising to this level is the development of consciousness or of a conscious mind. By *consciousness,* I mean the ability to call upon an observing self that can watch the mind's activities and help it to make choices about the quality of mental processes it engages in. This is easier said than done because we humans have a strong tendency to lose ourselves in the endless chatter of mental activity. Consciousness, in other words, is a disciplined practice that we must build through time by reminding ourselves over and over again to observe and guide our own minds.

Without this discipline, neither evolution nor self-determination is possible. We are overcome by the power of habitual ways of thinking, a power that derives in part from the conservation of energy that habits enable. Philosopher and quantum physicist David Bohm makes a distinction between "thoughting" and thinking.[3] For him, "thoughting" is the process of recycling thoughts we've had before—preexisting beliefs, assumptions, opinions, conventional wisdom, and truisms. Thinking, by contrast, is a relatively rare activity wherein we generate new thoughts. Without the exercise of conscious awareness and choice, we are condemned to endlessly cycling through old, predetermined patterns, making it nearly impossible to transform ourselves or our world.

*　　*　　*

By using the levels of paradigm as a framework that describes a hierarchy of value and potential, we avoid the mistake of treating these different perspectives as equivalent. They do *not* represent a menu of options that we can put on or take off at will as though no consequences follow from our choice. It matters very much which paradigm we adopt. Ultimately, as we are able to live at the higher levels, we also develop higher levels of consciousness.

CHAPTER TWO

Seven First Principles of Regeneration

I WAS BLESSED to have a grandfather, Noble Murray, who was half Mohawk on his mother's side and one quarter Mohawk on his father's side. His grandparents spent a great deal of time with him, and he did the same with me. Our lineage was through the Turtle Clan of his grandmother within a matrilineal social system. He told me stories about the ways she taught him to interpret the voices of nature and life.

As the result of a childhood illness, my grandfather stood at five feet two inches tall, and everyone called him Shorty. He may have been small in stature, but he was certainly not small in will. His father had left the reservation to gain some relief from the oppressive restrictions then placed on indigenous people by the federal bureaucracies that oversaw every aspect of their lives. Shorty's father told him, "You are the generation that is going to reclaim for us our indigenous ways." My grandfather was a farmer who never graduated from high school, but his understanding of natural systems enabled him to rise to the level of instructor within the newly formed agricultural extension system that was established in the early decades of the twentieth century.

These streams came together in the ways he taught my sister and me when we were quite young. With regard to his grandchildren, he wanted to live out what his father had charged him with, and he hoped that we would reclaim our indigenous identity. More important, he wanted us to be able to tap into indigenous ways of seeing and understanding the world. His methods were experiential, rather than didactic. I remember vividly, for example, how he taught me to raise pigs. He insisted that every hog, sow, and piglet have a name, because he wanted me to understand that each animal was different and needed to be cared for individually.

He also taught me to observe changes in the seasons and changes in the development of the piglets, so that I would know how to respond appropriately. He taught me that the pigs had a role, first as members of a working farm community and later as a source of food. Each day we would take the animals, who were as intelligent and well-trained as dogs, for a walk down to a favorite tree by the river, and the pigs would root up weeds as we went. Basically, he introduced me to a world of dynamism, flow, and change, within which each living creature must make its own individual response. It was a vivid world of differentiation and co-responsibility, and all living things had a place within it.

Inside, Outside, All Around

There was a rubric that informed my grandfather's teaching. He called it "inside before outside." He was referring to preparing the inside of myself before I sought to understand other people or outer circumstances. In other words, I had to prepare myself to see reality so that I didn't remain blinded by my own projections and fabrications. When I got myself in the right state of inner being, I would be able to see the outer world as it was really working. Between and all around these two ways of being, the inner and outer, was a third force. Shorty encouraged me to develop and grow my capacity to manage the interactions and relationships *between* inner and outer. From his perspective, developing this capacity was a person's most important work.

Inner Work

Later in life, I applied what my grandfather taught me when I was parenting my own two children. When they were young, I learned to pause before I jumped to engage with them, either to join in their joy or to correct them. I knew that I had to start with waking myself up if I wanted to avoid bringing a mechanical and unaware presence into their lives. There were some tricks for doing this that my grandfather passed down to me. I needed to image them as *whole*, independent beings who were pursuing their lives fully, growing more and more able to *contribute and learn*, and becoming more able to express the most *essential* aspects of themselves into the world.

I have come to think of this imaging process as a set of three practices or disciplines that enable me to become present and conscious of *whatever* I'm engaging with, experiencing it as alive and particular rather than in generic terms. This process makes it possible for me to see *any* being as a

1. *Whole* that has
2. *Potential* as the result it is own special being, and an
3. *Essence* that is like no other.

Of course, these practices apply to more than just raising children. I have strived to make this approach central to how I engage with everything. For example, when I work with a business, I start by thinking of it as a whole with a distinctive essence, filled with as yet unexpressed potential. As I work with the people in this business, I think of them in exactly the same way.

This also applies to natural systems, such as animals or watersheds. Each of these is a fully alive being, seeking to play its role within something larger than itself and imbued with an essence of its own. In other words, every living being is different from every other living being. When it comes to life, there are no categories or types. Each living system is singular.

Outer Work

In addition to inner work, my grandfather also taught me about outer work. This had to do with learning to perceive the subtle underlying dynamics that arise from the relationships of living beings to their world. I could see this very clearly with my children. To understand them well, I needed to see them not only in terms of who they were, but also in terms of how they interacted within our family, at school, with their friends, in the neighborhood, and so on. In other words, I needed to see them not as isolated beings but as nested within and having an effect on a larger whole, their living social and material context.

From an early age, both of my children were accustomed to taking on household tasks and chores of their own choosing. About the time they turned nine, I invited them to choose a household system that they wanted to manage on behalf of the rest of us, so that the family could work well together and each of us could pursue what mattered most to us. This gave them a critical role to play, based on something that deeply interested them and that they knew would help the family work better.

My son chose feeding us dinner; my daughter chose managing the family budget, including paying our bills and reconciling the checkbook. They knew that the work they had taken on was important to the other family members. When my teenage son was offered an internship at Lockheed, my daughter made sure there was a slush fund in the budget to cover his bus fares. In turn, when she began training as a gymnast, my son worked with her to develop menus that would support her athletic aspirations. As a single mom and sole breadwinner, I was greatly assisted by our collective intention to create a healthy family together.

Each of the kids was young enough to find this responsibility a thrilling challenge to their creativity, at the upper limits of their capacity. Yet they were frequently overwhelmed when they couldn't get things to work or figure them out. So we held a weekly Sunday meeting where we reflected on what they were learning, how they were growing, and why they loved the work they had chosen. This allowed them to start each week with a renewed sense of purpose and agency, and excitement about what they were going to do next. My friends were often astonished at the level of responsibility my children were willing and able to take on of their own accord. But I have always believed that this kind of self-generated creativity and accountability is inherent in human beings, so long as the right conditions can be provided.

Years later, I can see that I was expressing three more of my grandfather's lessons in the way I was raising my children. I was always seeking to support their agency and self-determination in the context of serving something larger than themselves by remembering that they were *nested* within a family and community. This gave them opportunities to make meaningful choices based on their own ability to discern what was important (or *nodal*), and it helped them reconnect on a regular basis to the energy *field* that was the source of their inspiration and motivation.

This anecdote reveals what I have come to see as a second set of three practices, oriented toward understanding how a living entity can successfully express itself and create beneficial effects within its context. From my grandfather, I learned to hold a dynamic image in my mind of the necessary sustenance that a living entity receives by being

1. *Nested* within and making contributions to a larger system, so that I can recognize how to intervene in ways that are
2. *Nodal* in order to produce a prime, higher-order effect that creates the conditions for beneficial growth, fostering as a result a
3. *Field* of creative energy that makes it possible for living beings to bring forth the best they are capable of, individually and collectively.

These practices may seem a little abstract, but they can be anchored to my story about my children. I was very careful *always* to see them nested within our family and social contexts. It was in this dynamic relationship that their full maturation became possible. The trick was to find the right nodal intervention, one that would stimulate their growth and development. I hit upon the idea of enabling them to choose the way they wanted to support the family as a whole and to nourish their ability to make wise choices. To keep this working, it was very important to sustain a creative energy field within which the systems they took on could remain sources of creativity and growth, rather than degenerating into a series of rote tasks and chores. This was the role of our Sunday meetings, which eventually evolved into almost daily conversations at the dinner table. They helped us re-inspire ourselves and one another with regard to the vital contribution each of us was making to the lives of the others, and they always ended by looking forward to what we were going to create next.

It may not be entirely obvious at first, but the point of these three practices is to keep ourselves connected to the inherent dynamism and change that comes from engaging with the world as a living place, filled with living, dynamic beings. All of us are alive and changing all the time; who we were yesterday is no longer necessarily who we are today. To understand ourselves, one another, and the world requires taking this dynamism into account.

But this is so easy to forget! How do we learn to begin every encounter by asking ourselves these questions:

- What are the conditions I will be working with today?
- How can they be harnessed to produce the growth that is desired?

It is important to remember that the ways we are nested into the systems around us are also changing. Additional questions are

- Who am I becoming now?
- How does that change the potential for relating to my environment?

What is nodal will also change, depending on the dynamics at play in each new situation, and energy fields are notoriously ephemeral. It takes a dedicated and consistent practice to maintain the motivation and aspiration that will allow individuals and communities to express the full range of their capability.

My ideas about child rearing had some of their origins in the educational ferment of the late 1960s and early 1970s. During the time when my children were quite young, I was heavily influenced by Joseph Campbell, who was teaching at the same university in San Francisco where I was a lecturer. I attended a series of his anthropological lectures in which he offered anecdotes and stories from tribes around the world.

Given my preoccupations as a young mother, I was particularly struck by what he said about indigenous child rearing. He described the role of extended families in helping children grow up to be contributing members of the tribe. The adults collectively observed the children, noticing how they played, what they were drawn to, and what they naturally stepped forward to participate in. For instance, as the adults were working, they would notice children watching and invite them to come and help. The children's responses told the adults much about their inclinations and opened the way to increasingly challenging opportunities for learning. Through this organic dance of call and response, the whole village participated in developing its children. I recognized in the archetypal tribal process that Campbell was describing the same approach that my grandfather had taken with me. I resolved to bring this approach to my own children.

All-Around Work

The last lesson from my grandfather, the one that makes the others hang together, came from his conviction that our foundational task as human beings is to be responsible for ourselves–to be self-determining. All of the other practices I've described won't amount to anything if we can't remember them and don't choose to use them! We have to learn how to take ourselves in hand, wake ourselves up, and grow our capacity to choose well for both ourselves and others.

I name this final, pervasive practice *development*, and I see it as the key to all of the others. The adults in Joseph Campbell's stories were seeking to develop the children of the village, not by telling them what to do but by inviting them to pursue their interests while guiding them in those pursuits through the stories and wisdom traditions of the culture. Thus, children were able to find ways to grow and develop by taking action in service to the community as a whole. This is what it took to enable them to emerge into full membership in the tribe, generation after generation. They could not be coerced. If the larger community was to remain healthy and resilient, it was imperative that its children be self-determining.

Once I learned this lesson for myself, I quickly realized that it applied to everything and everyone around me. Like me, everyone has the inherent ability and drive to develop—to express more of who they are and what they have potential to become. This drive may have been suppressed by personal history or cultural restraints, but I believe that it is a fundamental aspect of human nature that can be rediscovered and reawakened at any time.

Using these early thoughts as a platform for my own development, I've spent the better part of my career evolving my practice with regard to what development requires. Tapping into the developmental potential in people and organizations has been at the center of the change processes I've designed, and it is key to a non-heroic approach to world evolution. After all, the energy for change doesn't come from heroes. It lies within every living thing, waiting for the right opportunity to be expressed.

The practice of adopting a developmental perspective was threaded throughout the story about my children. I made a strong, conscious effort to use their upbringing as a way to foster their self-determination. They chose the arenas of responsibility and learning that were resonant for them. They evaluated their own progress and determined their growth trajectories. My task was to place opportunities before them and help them build an increasingly whole understanding of the implications of their choices. In spite of my own parents' old-school child-rearing, I knew better than to ever make my children's choices for them.

A Framework of Seven First Principles

Principles enable us to extend our thoughts and actions into new territory while building on insights and past experience. They allow us to free ourselves from slavishly copying what has been done before because they offer the fruits of experience distilled into general guidelines. When we apply them consciously, they open up a structured space within which flexibility and creativity remain anchored to reality.

First principles are the result of a disciplined process to dig down to the original or fundamental understanding from which all of our other principles derive. They are axiomatic: they can't be proven but our entire way of understanding the world flows from them. Philosophy, mathematics, and all of the sciences are built on the foundations of first principles, and great revolutions occur in these fields when one of these principles gets challenged. (For example, our understanding of space was radically altered when non-Euclidean geometry introduced the idea that parallel lines *do* meet at an infinitely distant point.)

The seven first principles that I am introducing here are meant to provide a foundational understanding of how regeneration occurs in living systems. On the one hand, they are rooted in emerging discoveries in ecology, psychology, general semantics, and other modern disciplines. On the other hand, they also have deep roots in ancient and indigenous ways of thinking.

The Seven First Principles of Regeneration Framework makes it easier to remember the seven principles and how they are connected. It is important to mention that each of these first principles points toward a way of thinking, from which different natures of activity can arise.

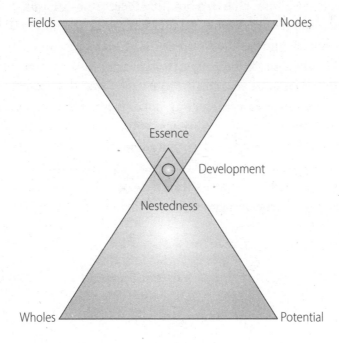

An Origin Story

People have asked me how I derived these principles, and I have had to admit that I don't know. They just seemed to show up, as though they were somewhere inside of me. But as I spent time thinking about them, I came to realize that they are in me precisely because my grandfather sought to teach them to me. Of course, he used very different language than I have come to use. Also, because his method was one of asking questions rather than telling me what I should think, his influence was subtle, deep, powerful, and lasting.

My grandfather's parents moved from the reservation shortly before he was born. They wanted to instill in their child a living relationship to his traditional culture, something that would be nearly impossible if he was surrounded by the oppressive control of the federal bureaucracy that was reshaping Native lives. By the time I came along, he was mostly called Shorty, but his father named him Noble because he wished to invoke the qualities for which the Mohawk people had once been famous.

Noble taught me in an indigenous way, through questions, stories, and understated humor. His overarching theme, the question that I most associate with him, was, "How did this come to be this way?" He wanted me to step back and see the world as living, dynamic, and coming into being. He wanted me to understand the energies at work in my life and to see that there was more going on than just my material circumstances. His central question served as a doorway, not only into the aliveness of things but also into the potential for aliveness within my own mind. Whenever I spent the night with him and my grandmother, he would ask me to tell him the story of how the events of my day had come to be the way they were. Over time, I learned from him the ways of observing and thinking that later revealed the first principles.

Seven First Principles of Regeneration Defined

Wholes

When I was ten, I had a crush on an older man of thirteen named Clint, a kid from the neighborhood. He was a bit of a bad boy, mischievous, neglected, and at least in my eyes, charismatic. My father, a harsh man in the best of circumstances, had nothing good to say about Clint, and he warned me that Clint was a bad actor who was going to end up in jail.

I brought each of my father's pronouncements about Clint to my grandfather, who gently challenged me to do my own thinking. "Okay," he would say, "but who is he really?" We lived in a small town, and my grandfather knew very well who Clint was. But he was interested in the boy's spirit, not his bad behavior. He explained to me that in the Mohawk tradition, thirteen was the age when young people chose their own names, names that expressed who they truly were. "If Clint were to give himself a name, what do you think he would call himself?" he asked me. He was subtly pointing out that my father had reduced Clint, a whole human being, down to a perceived character flaw. His question reminded me that we were speaking of a person.

Seeing wholes is important because it counteracts our mental tendency to fragment. It's actually easy to do, but it is a little hard to describe. Start by seeing something as it presents itself in its entirety, independent of any analysis—not as a collection of parts or characteristics, not in terms of its relationships, but simply as itself. When we begin from the image of a simple entirety, whatever we are looking at presents itself to our minds as singular, as just what it is. Later we can examine it for the multiplicity of inner and outer aspects and connections that are also true of it. But first we have to recognize that it just *is*, there before us as its singular self: a person, a city, a forest. This is the significance of the Mohawk naming tradition described by my grandfather. Before we begin to describe the dynamics, elements, characteristics, and problems of any given thing, we can pause and take in the fact of its primal reality, the *is-ness here in this moment* of it—a living whole that we encounter with our own whole being and can respect for its singular and independent existence.

Potential

Though Noble knew that my father had forbidden me to be friends with Clint, he nevertheless worked with me to understand this boy. I believe that he was intentionally tending my soul. He didn't want me to inherit the judgmental attitudes that characterized my father and his social set. He wanted me instead to understand who Clint was at his core, despite his difficult family and circumstances. What potential could he manifest were it possible for him to overcome these circumstances? What was in his heart that wanted to express itself? My grandfather's tutelage helped me move beyond my childish crush and learn instead to care about Clint.

Potential refers to the relationship between the inherent character or qualities of a whole (which are enduring) and how they could be called forth and expressed within a given context (which is continuously changing). This dynamic between what is enduring and what is changing means that there is always new potential to be discovered, developed, and realized for every whole in every situation. How energizing! This means that the world is filled with potential so long as we intend to engage it that way. Likewise, every aspect of our lives is filled with potential, if only we remember to seek it out and make it manifest. The secret is to care. Of course, this demands that we stay awake and not trick ourselves into believing that what we see around us is the only possibility. It requires developing ourselves to always look for the potential in any situation we encounter.

Essence

There was another important lesson embedded in the series of interactions between my grandfather and me about Clint. He was giving me hints of something very profound in Mohawk cosmology. If Clint had been a child from my grandfather's tribe, his adolescence would have signaled the moment for a rite of passage designed to help him transition from child to full membership in and responsibility for the tribe. For boys, these rites included ordeals of self-discovery through vision quests and the discovery of animal allies. Once a boy knew who he truly was and what he was called to be in this lifetime, he was in a position to choose his own name. My grandfather, in other words, was teaching me about the essences of people and things. This understanding—that everything has a unique energetic or spiritual core—was central to the way my grandfather viewed the world.

Essence is the irreducible core of something, what makes it singularly itself. To make this a little more concrete, let's apply it to people. Although I believe that every living entity has an essence, in general the concept is easier to grasp by narrowing it down to people. One way to differentiate our essence is to distinguish it from our personality.

Personality is the composite of traits and strategies that we acquire over time in order to function within society. Essence is prior to personality, what we are even on the day we're born. It's the aspect of ourselves that we refer to when we speak of wanting to get back to who we truly are, independently of the social pressures and constraints that push us to conform to the expectations of others. This irreducible core is what allows us to experience ourselves as integrated beings with coherent selves that endure even as we grow and change through our lifetimes. Learning to engage in essence thinking—to experience ourselves, our fellow humans, and everything around us in terms of essence—is foundational to understanding *wholes* and their *potential*.

Development

In these conversations about Clint, it's important to remember that my grandfather was working on developing something in me. He wanted me to become an independent thinker, capable of seeing things and people without sentiment or judgment, but with compassion and clear vision. His method was to ask me questions, not give me answers. His attitude was that of a farmer, a cultivator of humans and other living things.

A few years later, I was heartbroken to learn that at the age of sixteen Clint had been sent to prison for stealing cattle from my father. In my father's eyes, Clint had proven once and for all that he was a bad character, and this justified bringing the full weight of the law onto his head. In this regard, my father was in perfect alignment with the general beliefs of our culture—that people are bad (or stupid or lazy) by nature and that character is fixed and unchanging. But I knew in my bones that this wasn't true because I had experienced my own development through my relationship with my grandfather. As my many subsequent years in business and education have confirmed, all of us are always works in progress.

Development is the means by which essence becomes increasingly able to reveal and express itself as potential. For humans, development grows the ability to be self-determining, finding essence-sourced ways to contribute to the social and ecological systems to which we belong. As an approach, development is an alternative to the ideologies of command and control that are so pervasive in our social institutions—from parenting to education to business to government and religion.

In my experience there are three conditions that must be met if a process is to be developmental:

1. Development is intentional, not accidental. You have to design for it.
2. It occurs in a regular and recurring pattern. It is not ad hoc or occasional.
3. It is based on a coherent theory and methodology (a school of thought) for how living beings transform themselves in order to express more of their essence into the world.

Development demands two things of us.

We must start from recognition of the places where we are lacking capability, rather than always leaning on the capabilities we already have.

We must be willing, even enthusiastic, about taking on challenges and rising to them in ways that will inevitably require us to grow.

Nestedness

In the summer, my grandfather and I would gather special things to sell at his stand during the weekly market held on the town square. There were pecans from the wild trees along the river and wildflowers that bloomed in the meadows and fencerows. An enthusiastic child entrepreneur, I wanted to pick like crazy, inspired by my visions of making a killing at the market.

"Now let's think about this," my grandfather would intervene. "Who are these things for? Mother Nature has been growing everything for us, and she'll keep right on doing a good job of taking care of them, if we let her. So we should only take something that we know someone is going to want."

He was teaching me that I was part of something larger than myself— part of nature and part of a community. Customers weren't ideas with wallets; they were real people with whom I was connected. He wanted me to be as specific as possible about who they were and why they would want what I was bringing them. (As a happy by-product, I was able to honestly say to customers when I saw them, "I was thinking of you when I made this!" How could they resist?)

From my grandfather's perspective, we are all nested in context. He believed that if I was to have a happy and successful life, I was going to need to learn how to be in relationship with my context. I remember one instance of his teaching in particular. It was the week before graduation at the local high school, and we were trying to figure out why kids might want flowers to celebrate. "Would boys be willing to buy corsages for their girlfriends?" I pondered. My grandfather just gave me a look. "I know!" I suddenly exclaimed. "Parents will want to buy flowers for their kids to celebrate their big accomplishment." This idea satisfied him, and we went to recruit my grandmother to help. She pulled out Mason jars from storage and an old box of ribbons. We decorated the jars with ribbons and filled them with flowers, and they were an unqualified hit at the market. No one knew they were looking for a gift like this, but they were positively thrilled to find it.

Nestedness enables us to gain depth perception. Most people have some sense that everything in our universe is connected, but when they try to make use of this thought, they generally collapse into confusion and mental overload. Visualizing these infinite connections, they end up with a picture that looks like a plate of spaghetti. Understanding the world in terms of nested systems is a way out of this confusion. Not only are all things connected, but these connections are ordered into different *levels* of system. For example, individual humans are nested within social groupings such as families and communities, which are themselves nested within ecosystems. Each of these different levels requires a different kind of thinking in order to understand it and invites different natures of action in order to affect it.

Smaller systems can impact the working of the larger systems that contain them, and vice versa. Thus, individuals can have beneficial or destructive influence on the health of the social systems that they are nested within, just as social systems can support or undermine the well-being of individuals. Understanding this gives us much greater ability to be effective in carrying out our intentions, as long as we remain grounded in the reality of their context.

I came to understand nestedness quite vividly when I was working on a degree in psychology, studying family systems. Too often people try to fix a child when the real problem is with the family, which may in turn be struggling with problems sourced in its socioeconomic environment. Having a nested understanding gives us ways to make more realistic and practical choices about where and how to intervene in order to make a meaningful difference.

Nodes

My grandmother was a devout Christian who was determined to teach her unruly granddaughter to be considerate and thoughtful of others. It was a theme she repeated over and over with me, but it tended to go in one ear and out the other. In the years since, I've wondered why. I now know that it was because her admonitions on this one aspect of my behavior were uncharacteristically general and therefore abstract. She was upholding a Biblical code of conduct (a mental model), which never really connected with my childish concerns and enthusiasms.

My grandfather, on the other hand, plugged me directly into what it meant to consider someone else. When he taught me to know the pigs on the farm, to care about Clint, and to think about the person who would buy my flowers, he was teaching me thoughtfulness in a way that was immediately linked to everything that was important to me in life. In other words, he was able to discover the precise moments where interventions would make a difference in my development as a human being. He was always seeking to create an intentional shift in my perspective and to teach me how to do this for myself. It was a lesson that has served me throughout my life.

Nodes are like the keys to a system. They concentrate into a single concept or intervention the potential for transforming the whole of a system. Of course, this means we have to start from an understanding of the system as a whole, its character or essence, the ways it works, and the nested relationships that are driving its evolution. We also need to merge with the subject of our inquiry, experiencing it from the inside and surrendering all of our preconceptions about it. This enables us to perceive how the system is coming into being, to anticipate what is emerging and why. It requires thinking in a nodal way, scanning the patterns of activity or change for the highly charged places of concentration where something new can burst forth into existence.

This idea is subtly different from thinking about leverage, which is a mechanistic concept. When we look at leverage in a system, we think about how an action at one point translates into multiple effects in isolated parts of the system. When we think nodally, we look for the interventions to which the system as a *whole* will respond. An example in my children's education was helping my son identify cooking as his gift to our family. Cooking was a node that touched several key aspects of his life—his desire to contribute, to be creative, to manage complicated tasks, and to care for the people closest to him.

Fields

On reflection, I can see that my grandfather worked with me in ways that were deeply intentional and consistent. He grounded every lesson in an experience that was immediate, concrete, real, and personally relevant. He always invited me to be reflective, to slow down my tendency to jump straight into action and instead spend some time observing what was going on in me and the people around me. His questions almost always had the effect of enlarging my perspective, causing me to see things in a more systemic way and to choose actions that were likely to benefit everyone involved. You could say that my grandfather was interrupting my ordinary existence. It was almost as if he lived in a different world from me and from many of the people I knew, and when I was with him, he could open a door into that world for me.

Fields (a concept that shows up in both the physical and social sciences) are organized patterns of energy that influence and respond to the quality of activity occurring within a system. This implies that if we want to affect a system, the way to do so is by working on the energy field that is organizing it. Fields are one of the underlying conditions that make it possible to transform a whole system through a single nodal intervention.

Working on fields is a sophisticated practice, but the experience of them is commonplace. For example, we've probably all walked into a gathering, such as a family celebration, so contentious or chaotic that its original purpose is lost. What's needed is a way to shift the atmosphere (or energy field) so that something new becomes possible. Field shifting and reordering is an art that depends on all six of the first principles explored in this chapter. It is a powerful way to create the conditions for change, because fields are universal—all of us work and live within them. This means that the most powerful way to help people change their behaviors and the purposes they pursue is not to work on them individually, as if they were atoms scattered around at random, but to reshape the fields that bring them into energetic connection.

*   *   *

If our aim is to become regenerative in our lives, we need to learn how to apply these core principles of regeneration. This was the thrust of the education I received from my grandfather, and it was the basis of my exploration as I raised my children and developed my career working with businesses on strategic change. In the process, I acquired a wealth of experience with most of the difficulties, internal and external, that hinder the application of these principles.

To understand why the seven principles are difficult to apply in practice, it is useful to consider several impediments. To start, Western education simply doesn't value or address them, so our innate ability to practice them tends to atrophy. Also, our society teaches the opposite of these principles (for example, the common truism that in order to solve a problem we must break it down into its component parts). Consequently, we have a number of premises to unlearn in order to understand living systems.

Most challenging are the phenomena I call the *Six Internal Obstacles*, a set of basic human tendencies that distract or prevent us from seeing, thinking, and acting in beneficial ways. The idea of inner obstacles shows up in nearly every spiritual and humanistic school. For my purposes, I work with a set of six: fabrication, identification, waste, fear, attachment, and self-centeredness. Let's look at each obstacle in more detail to show what we may need to address.

Six Inner Obstacles to a Regenerative Life

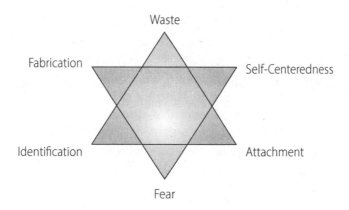

I have my grandmother, Valentine Murray, to thank for teaching me to become aware of these self-defeating aspects of my thoughts and behavior. Steeped as she was in the culture of the Southern Baptist church, she sought to instill values that are common to many spiritual and psychological traditions—humility, honesty, and self-accountability—which were often absent in my childish behavior.

Valentine was the de facto matriarch of our clan, and she oversaw the activities and social dynamics of the women's side of the family. It was customary when I was a child for rural women to come together to make quilts, put up the harvest, and talk over the challenges of child rearing. It was within this nurturing environment that my grandmother cultivated my self-awareness.

Valentine was an unusually effective teacher. Unlike the style of her church, which very clearly told its members what to do, she encouraged me to build my own moral compass. When she saw me acting out, rather than admonish me she would sit me down, take my hand between hers, and softly ask a question designed to get me to reflect on myself. Through her questioning, I learned to recognize and find ways to address my obstacles:

Fabrication. Like most children, I often made up or embellished my experience with stories that exaggerated the horribleness or wonderfulness of quotidian events. "Tell me, my dear," she would prompt, "are you making that up? Are you making it worse than it really was?"

Identification. I couldn't bear to be called names. I would fly into a rage or run and hide if someone asserted that I was something other than the good little girl I believed myself to be. "Are you taking this personally?" Grandmother would hint. "Maybe what they're saying is more about them than about you."

Waste. Not surprisingly, I was often heedless of the ways my plans and actions might affect the people around me. "Is that thought helpful?" Grandmother would ask me. "Can you see the effect you're about to have?"

Fear. Sometimes my father's brutality and my mother's incapacity would overwhelm me and I would panic. On these occasions my grandmother was particularly gentle. "Do you feel confused or scared right now?" she would suggest. "Do you want to figure out a way to work on this?"

Attachment. "Nothing is permanent" was a sort of mantra for my grandmother. In my child's mind, whatever I was feeling in the moment was the whole of reality, the only possible truth. Yet, as Valentine could so clearly see, the storm or enthusiasm would blow over, and soon I'd be onto something else. She would periodically point out the changes in my attitudes and state of being. "So your friend is the worst person in the world today?" she would observe. "That's funny. Yesterday she was the best! Your feelings changed a lot overnight, didn't they?"

Self-Centeredness. Valentine had a particularly low tolerance for self-centeredness in her grandchildren. Rural women of her class knew all too well how critical it was for people to be able to work together and depend on one another. "You don't think of anyone but yourself!" she would snap at me when I would launch into a tantrum over not getting what I wanted. "Is everything all about you?"

In her homespun way, Valentine Murray taught me a profound truth at a very early age—that it was possible to know myself and to make conscious decisions about how I responded to life's slings and arrows. Though it may be hard to manage these six obstacles, it is in fact doable. In my case, understanding of these early lessons took many years to ripen, but their presence in my childish experience meant that I always knew that I had a choice about who I could be. I believe this inner knowledge helped me survive and flourish, in spite of my family history of abuse and mental illness.

CHAPTER THREE

Regenerative Roles

AS I MENTIONED in chapter 2, I didn't grow up in a well-functioning nuclear family. My mother was mentally ill, a condition that also destroyed my younger sister as she got older, and my father was physically and emotionally abusive. It was my grandparents who truly cared for me and helped me lay the foundation for a sane and productive adulthood.

My grandfather learned early on that putting family and community ahead of oneself was the only way to survive, and he and my grandmother worked hard to teach me this critical lesson. My grandmother taught me the importance of thinking of others. I remember her shaking me by the back of my collar, like a mother wolf shaking her pups by the scruffs of their necks. "Don't you think of anyone other than yourself?" she admonished me. My grandfather took the lesson deeper. He wanted me to have a role in life, something that was helpful and meaningful and would give me an anchor from which to grow a sense of self. He wanted me to know that I was useful and worthy, and his gentle teaching served me well during the years when I was belittled by my father.

As I observed later, when I looked back at his approach, teaching a role goes beyond teaching good behavior, and it takes context into account. My grandfather's indigenous worldview always took into account some larger context and how he fit within it, and this is what he wanted me to learn to do. For example, no matter how hard he had worked at the farm during the day, the first thing he did when he got home was take off his jacket, roll up his sleeves, and go to my grandmother to ask if she needed help. He was small and skinny and she was big and round—they were the perfect image of Jack Sprat and his wife—and he adored her. In his mind, his role in the house was a supporting one, designed to enable her success in her role. It would never have occurred to him to think, "Well, I've done my work, so now I'm going to sit down and be served." That would have meant taking himself out of context and failing to play his necessary part.

A role is more than rote or habitual performance, a task list, or a job description. In order to serve a larger whole, a role has to be regenerated, made fresh and alive in the moment, every time it is played. Once you know the part that you need to play, you can invent the tasks that it will require. The role of parent, for example, can't be reduced to a list of activities, such as getting the kids fed and put to bed, although these activities might very well be called for. A role describes a relationship within a constantly changing context, and the tasks that it requires are also changing and unpredictable.

One day my grandfather and I might walk into the house and find my grandmother bent over the washtub, wringing out clothes. He would simply pick them up for her and carry them out to the line to hang them up. Or, if she was busy preparing supper, he would take over making the biscuits and gravy—one of his husbandly specialties. Somehow, even in the late 1940s and early 1950s, I got the unspoken message from him that a role was not determined by my gender, age, or status. It was a freely undertaken gift that I made of myself for the well-being of the whole, based on what was called for and what I could offer.

Nine Nodal Roles

Due to my grandfather's influence, I knew immediately when I set out to write a book about living a regenerative life that roles were going to be central to how I thought about the subject. More specifically, I wanted to understand which roles were critical to the regeneration of society and our world. What are the *nodal roles* that will allow us to endure and flourish as a species, and how do we learn to play them in a transformational way?

To assist me as I worked with this question, I chose to use as my framework an ancient, nine-pointed figure, called an *enneagram*, which can be used to understand the diverse forces that enable transformation. Based on the enneagram's underlying structure, I have organized these roles into three groups of three, in a framework I call the Regenerative Society Enneagram.

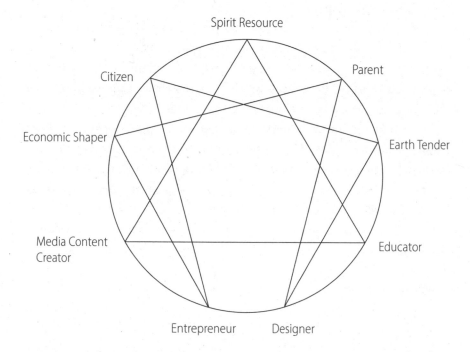

One group I call the *Initiators*. These are roles that create the conditions for growth and development by building the understanding and capability that living entities, such as children and farms, need in order to manifest their inherent potential into the world. I include in this group the roles of *Parent, Designer*, and *Earth Tender*

The next group I call the *Manifestors*. These are roles that seek to bring new ideas into concrete existence, to produce new value in the world. They do this by clearly imaging or articulating changes they want to introduce, why they want to introduce them, and for whom. I include in this group the roles of *Citizen, Entrepreneur*, and *Economic Shaper*.

The third group I call the *Destabilizers*. These are roles that help us learn how to manage uncertainty, a useful aspect of life when it disrupts the routine patterns of thought or behavior that keep us stuck in old ways. Destabilizers invite us to welcome and even pursue uncertainty in order to create the conditions for transformation. In this group I've placed *Educator, Media Content Creator* (such as blogger, journalist, or filmmaker), and *Spirit Resource* (for example, spiritual teacher, mentor, minister, and sometimes psychologist).

Obviously, these triads do not comprise all the roles that we play in life. There are, for example, many others whose purpose is to maintain continuity rather than to stimulate change. My intention in assembling these triads within the enneagram is to focus specifically on the forces that are core to social transformation.

I want to emphasize that the triads are not meant to form a typology. I don't mean to imply that we are by nature born into one or another of them. In fact, I mean to affirm just the opposite. Many—or perhaps most—of us play more than one of these roles in our lives. The point here is to develop the conscious understanding of their meaning and systemic importance that is necessary if we want to play them in a regenerative way.

The Initiator Triad

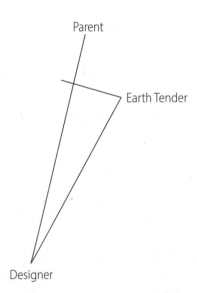

There is an internal set of relationships that pulls together the roles described in each of my triads, just as there is a larger set of relationships among the triads. This is what I've tried to capture in the titles I've given each of them. In this case, the title *Initiator* points to those roles that *prepare the conditions for change* to be introduced into the world.

The Regenerative Parent

The *Regenerative Parent* role is fundamentally concerned with guiding the development of *agency* in children. Children are, of course, born with agency, but at first it is mostly directed toward themselves: "Give me what I want!" The art of parenting is to help strengthen this sense of inner authority, while also helping children direct it toward purposes beyond themselves. This enables them to become self-managing, contributing members of society. Sadly, too many of our received notions about parenting either kill this spark or fail to give it appropriate shape and focus.

The Regenerative Designer

The *Regenerative Designer* role serves the creative aspirations of people, the desire to make something new. We could say that the designer gets called into being as soon as someone's agency has been awakened. Once people can see what they would like to manifest, they are immediately faced with questions of how. This is where the designer steps in. Nearly everything in our world requires or would benefit from design. This includes the physical objects we live with (such as furniture and clothing), the infrastructures we rely on (transportation and telecommunications), and the processes that enable and enrich our lives (banking or educating or cooking).

Yet great design is relatively rare, perhaps because so few people understand designing's inner demands. These include the ability to seek out and hold the cognitive tension that lies between the core potential hidden within people's pursuits and the core characteristics of their materials. These demands also include a willingness to enter the nonattached states that allow insight and the patience to wait for elegant solutions.

The Regenerative Earth Tender

The *Regenerative Earth Tender* role teaches us all how to fit within the laws and dynamics of living systems. Earth tenders read and interpret nature's patterns, seeking ways to align their actions with them. This role often gets expressed in careers or hobbies that involve being in nature, such as farming or forestry or gardening or being an amateur naturalist. What distinguishes regenerative Earth tenders is a passionate commitment to understanding how nature works and the ableness to translate this understanding into better decision making for themselves and society as a whole.

The Manifestor Triad

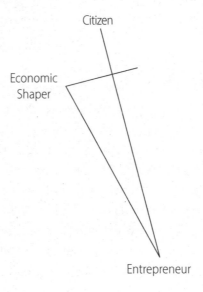

I have named the next set of three roles the *Manifestors*. While initiators create the conditions for change, manifestors engage directly with producing the effects of change in the world. They seek to create objects and systems, either because these objects and systems are missing or because they are possible.

The Regenerative Citizen

The *Regenerative Citizen* role takes responsibility for the creation of a healthy working society. Citizens engage with and shape the systems that govern their lives—such as governments, corporations, and community organizations—educating themselves to make sound decisions about them. Even within systems where decision making has been turned over to a representative body or board, citizens retain the rights and responsibilities of their role. These include

- Generating new thinking about the direction a society should take
- Developing in themselves and others the capacities needed to participate in an evolving and self-governing society
- Choosing representative leadership and being prepared to offer such leadership
- Monitoring and contributing to the quality of decisions being made
- Taking corrective action when improvements in governance are required

By definition, a citizen is an active, generative, and thoughtful participant.

The *Regenerative Entrepreneur* role drives social evolution by disrupting existing patterns of material life. An entrepreneur seeks to replace a given good or service with something that does a better job of allowing customers and other stakeholders to pursue their aims and purposes. The energy that gets released when entrepreneurs are able to harmonize their personal agency with the unmet aspirations of a market can be enormous and world-changing.

The Regenerative Economic Shaper

The *Regenerative Economic Shaper* role creates and refines the structures that allow societies to generate wealth in an enduring, equitable, and wholesome way. Economic shapers use a variety of instruments to carry out this purpose, such as policy, financial institutions, foundations, and economic development. In the context of regeneration, *wealth* refers to the capacity to influence and participate in processes that continually upgrade the well-being of individuals, communities, and ecosystems. By this definition, a society that enables every one of its members to participate in wealth creation will experience a virtuous cycle of accelerated evolution.

The Destabilizer Triad

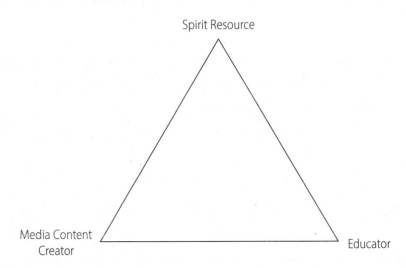

The last set of three roles is named *Destabilizers* because their task is to question, challenge, and even apply shocks to the status quo. Without this kind of intervention, people, organizations, communities, and nations can become rigid and reactionary, unable to summon the resilience and creativity they need to thrive in a changing world.

The Regenerative Educator

The *Regenerative Educator* role develops the ability of individuals to understand themselves and the world. Even more important, an educator helps people overcome their mental inertia—the strong human tendency to rely on old habits of thought and belief. True education is not about filling people up with information or knowledge. Instead, it's about enabling them to generate new thoughts that allow them to create meaning from what they know and to make wise and conscientious choices based on what's happening in the present moment. People are forever changed by truly educational experiences because through them they gain access and influence over their own minds.

The Regenerative Media Content Creator

The *Regenerative Media Content Creator* role surveys the overwhelming complexity of the world in order to discern and direct attention to what's important. Media content creators—who include everything from writers to filmmakers to song writers to journalists to newscasters to bloggers—produce stories or meaningful narratives in order to help us distinguish relevant information from noise. When the role is played at a regenerative level, it invites us to receive these stories with a critical, creative mind, putting them to use to find pathways toward hope and life-generating outcomes.

The Regenerative Spirit Resource

The *Regenerative Spirit Resource* role reconnects us (as individuals, communities, and nations) to the source of our will, vitality, energy, hope, and capacity for awe. Those people who take on this role help us to elevate our spirits when we feel low, and they remind us to bring the gifts of spirit into the way we live. They continually ask the big questions: *Why are we here? What does it mean to be human? What is our place in the universe? How should we live in order to fully manifest human potential?* Because they know that sleepwalking through day-to-day existence kills spirit, they admonish us: "Wake up!" This requires them to be masters of disruption, and it imposes on them a heavy responsibility to keep themselves awake. If we take on this role, we cannot serve the spiritual development of others if we haven't done the work ourselves.

Regenerative Roles at Work in the World: The Action Research Protocol

The Regenerative Life is the result of an action research project, which I undertook in order to more fully understand the nine regenerative roles as they appear in the world today. An action research project differs somewhat from traditional scientific research. In action research, subjects are not kept ignorant of the project's purpose and methodology in order to protect its objectivity. Instead, in a completely transparent process, they are invited to be active participants and to interpret results as they occur. In this way, researcher and subjects learn together, and the project offers immediate benefit for both. In recent years, action research has been widely adopted in both academic and business contexts as a way to create new knowledge.

Prior to this project, I spent more than 40 years working with companies to unleash their regenerative potential by developing their people's agency, creativity, and will in the context of changing the way they did business. I learned a lot about humans and regeneration within the business world, and I observed the ways that changing the challenges people took on at work changed who they were in all the other parts of their lives.

For this book, I wanted to come from the other side in order to demonstrate that people can make meaningful contributions to their worlds by elevating the primary roles they have chosen to play in all aspects of their lives. You don't need an enlightened work setting to grow yourself as a person, although it can be helpful. What you do need is the will to do more with your life, the courage to examine yourself, and people who share your methodology and are able to engage in reflection with you. These were the conditions I set out to create for the research project.

In 2018–2019, a self-selected group of 92 participants came together with me online for a series of workshops, exercises, and interviews that took place over six months. During this process, I was able to test my idea that by shifting the way we think about and play roles, we can significantly change the outcomes and levels of impact arising from how we engage in all kinds of situations. We were able to track how people's approaches to given roles changed when they had the opportunity to go through a structured learning process, applying the frameworks introduced here to their own lives and work.

I thought it was important to include diverse perspectives, and so I made sure that the much larger group that I and others reached out to for volunteers included men, women, and transgender people from many races and nationalities and was equally diverse in age, income, profession, and physical ability. What the final group of 92 all had in common was a desire to make their lives more meaningful and impactful with regard to the roles they already actively played.

I conducted an independent workshop series for each of the nine roles, but all had the same concept and structure. I introduced a disruption, a way of thinking that helped participants realize that the ways they have been playing their roles severely limit the desired effects that they can produce. Based on this, I asked them to apply what they learned in an event where they were called on to play their role, to observe the effects, and then to try again in a new event. They repeated this pattern of experimentation three times in order to assess the effect of the shift in their thinking and approach. Finally, I asked them to keep a journal of what was happening to allow them to reflect on and solidify the changes they were experiencing.

To create the desired shift in perspective, I asked participants to apply the following frameworks as a way to help them upgrade the performance of their role.

- *Levels of Paradigm.* They determined the paradigm they were currently operating from and how to move themselves up to the Regenerate Life Paradigm.
- *Seven First Principles of Regeneration.* They used the first principles to assess the coherence and wholeness of their choices and actions.
- *Inner Obstacles.* They observed energy drains that were undermining their efforts at improvement and articulated them in terms of inner obstacles.

Based on this work, I invited participants to set personal aims to help them maintain consciousness of the changes they wish to make in how the play their roles going forward. In addition, they kept journals of their experiences, recording the challenges, surprising results, and insights that occurred during this process. Written observation and reflection not only helped them anchor and retain the learning that occurred; it also provided the basis from which I drew the stories in the following chapters.

In sharing entries from these journals, my purpose is to show how many different possible approaches there can be to the non-heroic journey.

The frameworks I've introduced are intended to open up our options, so that each of us can approach our roles from our own essence and creativity. After all, the last thing I want to do is to encourage the idea that there is only one correct way to play any of these roles.

Because these are journal entries rather than crafted stories, they almost always describe inner, reflective processes, rather than outward series of actions and effects. This unusual emphasis might at first seem odd to some readers. However, it serves the useful purpose of redirecting our attention to changes in participants' patterns of thought and attitude, which requires a corresponding shift in what we consider interesting. Readers who are trying out the frameworks and exercises for themselves, and keeping their own journals of reflections, will experience the strongest resonance with the journal entries shared here.

Needless to say, it takes more than a brief series of workshops or reading and absorbing the content of this book to integrate the new ways of living called for by the Regenerate Life Paradigm. Deep change requires more than knowledge. It takes ongoing inner work to build the capability to evolve oneself and engage with life differently. I am suggesting an extremely effective way to launch this ongoing life's work: set an aim, attempt to apply it, and then reflect on how to improve. If nothing else, this simple, regenerating process always reawakens our will and gives us a pretty good picture about what in ourselves we need to work on. Let's get started!

CHAPTER FOUR

The Regenerative Parent Role

I T ISN'T AN ACCIDENT that I begin with the role of parent. Parenting is the foundational process from which we create the basis for societies to emerge, endure, or evolve. And, of course, I don't limit the role of parent to birth parents. Any of us who interact with children have opportunities to provide good parenting, if we know the role's meaning and aim and are willing to be generous with our time and energy toward the young people in our lives.

Societies concentrate the resources needed to create systems for developing and amplifying human potential. They serve the essential purpose of linking individuals together in ways that enable them to become more than they could be on their own. Through social participation and interaction, we find that our lives gain meaning and our actions gain significance. Ultimately, societies are the means we use for discovering how to consciously contribute to the evolution of life on Earth.

Child-rearing lays the groundwork for all other social processes. Parents help children grow their capacity to join with others in order to pursue common purposes. They do this by assisting their children to learn, understand, and value the social agreements that allow cooperation among people with widely diverging interests and goals. This can happen within the structure of a family, among a cohort of playmates, or in other social contexts. The point is to help children become contributing members of something that is bigger than they are and that serves a larger purpose.

The quality of these contributions depends in part on how well children come to know and manage themselves. Really great parenting is not only about helping children become socialized. It is also about helping children tap into and express in the fullest possible way their own potential.

Taken together, these two dimensions of parenting provide an engine for social evolution. Ideally, each generation passes down the collective wisdom of all prior generations about what it takes to get along and work together, and about what the consequences are for failing to do so. At the same time, each generation is encouraged to discover and express its own genius, adding new experience and insight to the collective wisdom. Naturally, this process isn't direct and linear. Societies come together and they fall apart, they improve and they regress, but the overall arc of history, to paraphrase Martin Luther King, bends toward justice.

A Small Caveat

My purpose here is to lift the role and practice of parenting up to the regenerative level, and this is what I will specifically address. At the same time, I recognize that there is a rich substrate of fundamental capabilities that make regenerative parenting effective. These include qualities such as love (or *caritas*, the love that has no opposite), nurturing, an ability to be present, an ability to discover and evolve appropriate boundaries, and a willingness to provide for the basic physical and emotional needs of children in ways that are appropriate to their stage of development. These qualities also include the willingness to learn. As a friend of mine once put it, "Parenting has been the greatest personal challenge of my life—I need to continually grow myself just to be able to stay ahead of my son!"

A careful reader will see all of these qualities and more exhibited in the stories and quotations from journals that follow. I don't speak to the qualities directly—not because I don't value them, but because I assume them and am inviting you to look beyond the horizon and see that even more is possible.

Experiencing the Regenerative Parent Role

Farmer and storyteller Lily Kellogg Hollister aspires to raise her daughter, two-year-old Eve, in a way that respects Eve's unique spirit. Lily recently shared with me an incident that came up while she was participating in my regenerative life research project. Her family was staying in the home of another family, whose three-year-old daughter, Viva, began bullying Eve—hitting her, pulling her hair, and yelling at her. All of the adults in the household struggled to find ways to address the situation as it played out over several days. This gave Lily an opportunity to observe and reflect on the various approaches and strategies she and the others brought to this developmental moment.

She watched how the other adults went into problem-solving mode and was aware that if she hadn't been part of the action research project, she would have gone there herself. She could see them attempting to exercise control over Viva's behavior, insisting that she obey and chastising her for her lack of self-control. She watched Viva's parents struggling with embarrassment over her behavior, identifying her aggression as a crisis that needed to be resolved. They were clearly worried that Viva's outbursts reflected badly on them as parents. She also saw the adults attempt to encourage Viva to show kindness toward Eve or to distract the two children by creating games where conflict was unlikely to arise.

Lily reported in her journal that when she reflected on what she had observed, she was able to recognize the paradigms that these actions were coming from (Arrest Disorder and Do Good) and to engage her friends in conversations that would evoke a more regenerative approach. "Why do you suppose Viva is acting out?" she asked them. "Is she overtired? Missing her dad when he's gone during the day? Jealous? What is she trying to express through her behavior? Thinking of her as a bad kid doesn't help us understand anything about what's going on with her." Hitting and yelling, Lily reflected to herself, are completely normal in very young children. Here is how she described the situation in her journal:

These girls are right at the point of learning all the complex, unwritten rules about engaging with others, and they are supposed to be testing boundaries right now. They are developmentally right on track. I need to learn how to help them build the ability to observe themselves so that in time they'll be able to reflect on their own behavior instead of having their parents reflect for them. I can't do this in the heat of the quarrel. It's as though I have to create a separate, quieter learning space, where reflection can be experienced. I also am really beginning to understand what is meant by the suggestion to reflect on *myself* in order to understand why certain behaviors trigger *me*. My task is to grow my capacity as a mother to respond developmentally to the rapidly evolving circumstances of the children in my care.

The Essence of the Regenerative Parent

For me, Lily's experience beautifully illustrates the essence of the regenerative parent role. First of all, she could see how important it is to create a learning space within which children can express, reflect, grow, and become responsible for themselves. At the same time, she was able to witness the strength with which lower orders of paradigm exert an influence over the thinking and choices of adult caregivers. After all, the parenting we know most intimately is the parenting we grew up with. For this reason, I believe that Lily was genuinely glad that I was able to share with her a framework for thinking about the essence of parenting at the regenerative level.

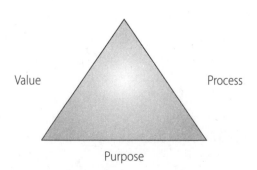

Value   Process

Purpose

The framework has three aspects. *Process* has to do with what is being done and how. *Purpose* has to do with why. *Value* has to do with the effect created in the world.

With regard to the Regenerative Parent Essence, I believe the process is to *evoke self-determination*. Lily's insight was quite powerful and somewhat counterintuitive—she needed to support the developmental need of children, even very young children, to make their own choices. As a parent, she needed to rein in her own strong desire to make choices for them and instead provide opportunities to help them learn to make better choices.

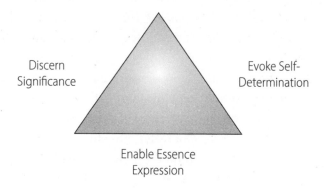

Discern Significance

Evoke Self-Determination

Enable Essence Expression

I believe that the development of this capability should begin when children are very young. By the time they hit puberty, their hormones and brain chemistry demand that they explore, take risks, and break rules. When they approach age fourteen or so, if they haven't developed the ability to manage themselves, make their own choices, and accept the consequences of these choices, their lives may actually be at risk. Happily, self-determination will serve people throughout their lives, regardless of the roles they choose to play. Indeed, it is a prerequisite to living a regenerative life. This is why the work of parenting is foundational to the kind of societal change that this book seeks to foster.

The regenerative parent role's purpose is to *enable essence expression*. One key to leading a meaningful life is the ability to know who we are and the overarching purpose we are pursuing. In other words, in order to be self-determining, we need to have some sense of the self that is doing the determining.

Lily's intervention in the adults' responses to the conflict between Viva and Eve displayed a subtle grasp of this idea. Each of the girls needed her own space for reflection in order to come to a sense of herself. Both were at the age when a child begins asking (endless!) questions, exhibiting curiosity and an effort to make sense of the world. Lily introduced simple, *reflective* questions: What happened? How did you feel? What did you want to do? And these questions suggested something new for the children to be curious about: Who am I? How do I feel about this? What are the ways that I want to respond? Although, as a two-year-old, Eve is too young to answer these questions now, they have been added to her repertoire, and throughout her childhood, her parents will continue to ask them. Soon enough she will become adept at recalling and thinking about them, and proposing answers to herself.

The value that flows from the regenerative parent role is *discern significance*. It is important to help children understand not only who they are but also the effects they have on the world around them, so that their development of agency is balanced by learning to take others into consideration. For children to understand the significance of their choices and actions, they must be able to accurately envision the impact they have in other people's lives. As this capability develops in children over time, they also develop ever more nuanced understanding of what actions are most likely to provide beneficial contributions to the causes they choose to serve.

Eve and Viva, as young as they were when this interaction took place, could still begin to wrestle with questions of how their actions were affecting others: What did Viva feel? What did Eva feel? Why do you think she felt that way? Could you do something else to make a different feeling happen? Moreover, Lily understood that these were relevant questions for both children. Through her bullying, Viva was creating an obvious effect. And Eve, by being a victim, was also producing an effect. Lily was quite conscious that simply stopping the bad behavior would do nothing to shift this underlying dynamic. She needed to help each of the children begin to see the effect they were having on the other and to help them understand what it felt like to be the other. Even more important, Lily needed to help the other parents discern the significance of the choices they were making in terms of the future development of these children.

Finding the Right Level

Rachel Kastner is based in San Miguel de Allende, Mexico, where she works in the fields of regenerative agriculture and supply network development. She and her daughter, Nayeli, a strong-willed and independent girl, were participants in the regenerative life research project.

When Nayeli turned three, she began to express her independence by resisting her mother's instructions, locking the two of them into an escalating battle of wills. Rachel reported that her instinct, based on deeply entrenched patterns from her own upbringing, was to become increasingly authoritarian. She feared that if she didn't lay down the law, her daughter would develop undesirable character traits. Nayeli's reaction was to dig in her heels, becoming more and more resistant to her mother's demands.

Rachel knew that this was not the kind of relationship she wanted with her child, but she simply couldn't find a way out. Within this context, her first encounter with the Levels of Paradigm Framework came as a revelation. "I realized that I was operating from the arrest disorder paradigm," she reported, "and it was beginning to damage the close and peaceful relationship that Nayeli and I had always enjoyed."

Rachel resolved to shift to a more regenerative approach. She gave herself a simple practice: whenever she observed Nayeli resisting something she was asked to do, she would rein in her tendency to repeat the request. Instead of upping the pressure, she taught herself to simply wait and observe. In one of her first experiences with this new approach, she asked Nayeli to put on her socks because they needed to get ready to leave the house. As Rachel reported later,

> Nayeli continued to play and seemed to ignore me. I stuck to my aim and restrained myself from making an immediate demand that she please put her socks on now. I simply observed her. After a short while, she got up and went and put her socks on by herself. I was shocked.

This pattern repeated itself, and Rachel began to understand that Nayeli, who was pursuing her own aims, was also perfectly happy to accommodate her mother as long as she didn't apply demands and pressure. Nayeli, Rachel soon realized, was attempting to express her own agency, to work through something that she was creating from her own mind.

> I think she was authentically finishing a task and would do what I asked very soon. She actually really cares about the house she is making for her toy dog and wants to complete the project. I discovered that insisting is usually unnecessary. My expectation for a child to respond the second a parent says something was silly. I wasn't seeing Nayeli for who she really was. It's only now that I can appreciate and be grateful for the fact that she didn't just buckle under to her mom's will.
>
> Instead of feeling like I'm on a distant level above her needing to keep rule—in other words, to arrest disorder—I feel more in tune with her. I notice I have to stop my own agenda to really connect with her and honor her being. I'm not just a mom running the schedule. What I want us to be are two dance partners who have built a relationship so that we can move through our days together. I know different preferences, priorities, and wants will generate some conflict along the way, but as long as Nayeli is learning how to balance being self-determining and being in relationship with others at the same time, I'm sure we can navigate those conflicts.

Applying the Seven First Principles

Brandi is a shy ten-year-old on the outside, a wildly expressive and artistic spirit on the inside. His dad, David Ray—an accountant at a firm near Seattle that assists small start-up businesses—had agreed to adopt him when he and his wife were unable to have children of their own. A traditionally conservative Christian household, they adored their new toddler, but they were poorly equipped to handle the situation when they began to realize that Brandi, whom they had originally named Brandon, did not fit within socially accepted gender norms. Brandi has recently requested that his parents change the name they call him (although he continues to refer to himself as a boy). He is artistic, and he likes to play dress-up and physically express himself through tumbling and dance, where he can be flamboyantly entertaining.

David joined the research project on the recommendation of a friend who knew that he was deeply troubled by the contradictions he was facing as he raised Brandi. Not only was Brandi affected by the stress of being adopted (he had been prescribed medication for anxiety when he was four), he was also now struggling with his differences from other boys. Meanwhile, David was struggling with his own gender biases, along with confusion surrounding how to reconcile the love he felt for his child with the teachings of his conservative church. His sense of confidence in his own ability to be a good father was being deeply challenged.

David's significant breakthrough came when we began to work with the Seven First Principles of Regeneration. He realized that he needed to see Brandi not as a problem child, not as a collection of symptoms (shyness, anxiety, effeminacy), but as a *whole* person with a unique *essence* and a powerful drive to express himself. David began to redefine his responsibility as a parent away from ensuring that Brandi conformed to social expectations and toward helping him burn as brightly as his *potential* clearly suggested he could.

With this recognition came a deeper insight into the way Brandi was *nested* into his family. David loved his son, but he always saw himself as a substitute father. He was very clear that Brandi had been born outside of the family, and he was doing his best to step in and provide a nurturing home. But when David checked with his wife, he was surprised to learn that she had no such qualifications. Brandi was her son and she was his mother—end of story. David realized that he was holding a fragmented view of his family and that it, too, needed to be approached as a whole. This subtly shifted the level of investment he was able and willing to make in Brandi's development.

David also began to recognize that the source of Brandi's anxiety had nothing to do with his ability to succeed, either as a student or as a kid. It came from constantly having to defend himself against a barrage of criticism and pressure to conform. Even when the pressure was subtle, it was pervasive. Thus, David realized that the most effective *nodal* intervention he could make in Brandi's life now was to provide environments where he would no longer need to fight so hard. Brandi needed to be in an energy *field* where his differences would be accepted and nourished. David and his wife found a school that specializes in working with children who don't fit into conventional settings, a school where kids direct their own learning and develop the skills needed to negotiate and work successfully with others.

During the course of the research project, David also undertook a little project with Brandi, one that was *developmental* for both of them. Brandi had found a box of his grandmother's old clothes in the garage, and he enjoyed assembling outfits from them to wear around the house. By this point, David had learned to restrain what he described in his journal entries as "my freak-outs," reminding himself instead to look for his child's essence. "What's going on here?" he asked himself. "How is Brandi expressing who he really is?"

After a couple of days of observing Brandi and talking with him about this new activity, David became aware of a pattern, which he confirmed with his wife.

"I thought Brandi was just playing dresss-up," he told her, "but it looks to me like he's actually creating something. It's as though he's reworking the clothes to make something new."

"Now that you point it out," she responded, "I think you're right. He's experimenting creatively. He's actually playing with fashion."

David tested this with Brandi. He asked, "Would you like to make your own clothes?"

Brandi lit up with palpable excitement. So they experimented. David found a company that prints customers' painted images on fabric and creates simple tunics. David and Brandi downloaded the company's template and got out some paints. Then David sat with his son for two hours of joyful immersion, free from the anxiety and lack of focus that so often troubled Brandi. When the garment came back in the mail, it was professionally wrapped in tissue in its own box—thrilling!

They looked at the results together. "What's next?" David inquired. "What do you want to create for your next project?"

Brandi studied his work. "Well, there are too many colors in it," he reflected. "I want to make the next one simpler. And I want to put a label in it: "Made by Brandi."

Managing Inner Obstacles

In each story I read from the regenerative parenting participants, there was at least one characteristic obstacle that they could recognize as an unconscious behavior pattern undermining what they were trying to accomplish as mothers and fathers. Managing these obstacles became part of their own inner development work.

Anastasia Smith is a project director for the White Buffalo Land Trust in Santa Barbara, California. Her story offers a perfect example of handling obstacles, one that almost every parent of young children will recognize. She reported on a trip to the grocery store with her five-year-old daughter, Phoenyx:

> Sometimes the grocery store seems like a gauntlet. The candy displays are specially designed to grab the attention of little ones. If you say "not today," then you're set up for tears or tantrums right there, where the entire world has to listen to them.
>
> Before I joined the regenerative life project, my strategy when this would occur was to get through the shopping as quickly as possible or give up altogether and run for the exit, overwhelmed by the feeling that I was being judged. It was so easy to imagine what others might be thinking: "She must not be a very good parent!" or "Why is that poor child crying? Why isn't her mother stopping her?" I knew that I wanted to change this overwhelming experience. From the project, I had learned that I was going to need to set an aim for myself, something I could remember when things were falling apart. I came up with, "Bring Myself Present!" because it was obvious that whatever I was imagining about how people might be thinking of me, it was pulling me out of what was actually happening in the moment.
>
> During a recent meltdown, I had an opportunity to use this aim to shift the pattern and step into the way I truly want to play my role as parent. Phoenyx had had a long day at school. I picked her up at school, asked how her day was, and then shared the laundry list of errands we had to do. We always talk in the car about what happened during the day, but that day she was irritable and surly. She had fought me getting

into the car, didn't want a hug, and began trying on an attitude learned from playmates.

When she realized which store we were at, she demanded a treat. I pointed out that her tone and way of asking didn't merit one. Oh, she was furious. She howled and cried and hit the sides of the cart while I attempted to throw a few things in for the weekly meals.

And then I stopped. I looked at her. I looked around me. I thought about the way I was starting to get worked up and realized that this was a trigger, an indicator that I needed to remember my aim. "Bring myself present!" I reminded myself. I knew that I needed to be present with Phoenyx, not with the other people in the store and my sense that they were judging me.

In that moment, I couldn't possibly know what everyone else was thinking about me as a parent. I was *fabricating* these stories, and this was amplifying my frustration with my daughter. I simply let go of my fantasy about how others might perceive me and suddenly I could focus on being with her. We could finish up our grocery shopping and step into a new space together because *I* had shifted my energy.

When we had loaded our groceries into the car and buckled ourselves in, Phoenyx said, "I'm sorry Mama. I love you. Can we go home and do something together?" The rest of the errands didn't feel that important, and we left them for another day.

On reflection, I realized that because I had arrived with an agenda that was important only to me, I had missed what she was needed—time for just the two of us. She needed to recalibrate with Mom after a long and—as I learned later—challenging day. She needed to be held and talked with in a quiet moment when there wasn't a next thing to do.

Phoenyx is a bright person, full of energy, who draws, play-acts, dances, works with her friends, and lives within a tightly scripted schedule at school. What she seeks is the space to connect one-on-one in a quiet moment with no agenda at the end of the day. This seems to be how she recharges her wellspring and zest for life. So I've shifted my patterns. Now I pick her up from school a little bit later so that I can go to the store first. Then we get to go straight home and draw or play outside or curl up with a book.

At a deeper level, I realize that in that moment when I shifted myself in the grocery store, I enabled her to *choose* how she wanted to respond to the "No Treat" situation instead of trying to make her act a certain way. This allowed her to be in her own process, and she came out of it wonderfully. When I let go of my own unnecessary and imaginary constraints, I opened the space for my daughter to discover a response that was true to her.

Generating a New Pattern

Each of the participants in the regenerative life research project went through a similar process. They came to understand what a different level of parenting would require of them. They evaluated how they were doing and where their obstacles typically showed up. They then worked on creating new patterns for themselves, along with aims that would help them remember to adopt the new pattern.

In the case of Zac Swartout—entrepreneur and cofounder of SuperAlloy Interactive in Vancouver, British Columbia—this meant completely reconceiving his role as a stepfather. Zac co-parents two lively teenagers, Sophie (aged fourteen) and Solomon (aged sixteen). He married their mother when they were younger, with the clear intention to become a fully engaged part of their lives. It wasn't long before he ran into trouble as the result of patterning his behavior on the ways he had been parented.

Zac's parents believed that their duty was to instruct their children. Whenever Zac faced some dilemma or challenge, his parents were ready with suggestions (or, on occasion, demands) about how the trouble should be handled. But when he tried out this approach on his stepchildren he discovered two things. First, he felt uncomfortable pretending that he always knew the right thing to do. Second, these kids didn't take well to instruction.

Sophie and Solomon had always been raised with an emphasis on the Socratic method. Their mom gave them a lot of room to make their own decisions, supported by insightful questions from her. She offered advice when asked, but generally she tried to get them to think for themselves. As intelligent and independent young people, they weren't looking for their stepdad to tell them what to do.

This was the question that Zac brought into the research project: "How can I find an engaged and engaging way to parent teenagers that provides them the support they need without telling them what to do?"

It so happened that I had dinner with Zac and his children during this time, and we talked about this question. I asked Solomon what he thought, and he told me that as he was being given more freedom, he wanted to know how to make good decisions, decisions that wouldn't get him into trouble or situations where he could get hurt. "I don't want to be told what to think; I want to *learn how* to think," he told us.

"Well, what do you think about that, Zac?" I asked. "What if you were to be completely transparent about how you were thinking about things, including all of the uncertainties and insecurities that come with trying to make good decisions? What if you were able to show Solomon the process you go through, including the frameworks you use to bring clarity to your thinking?"

Zac paused for a moment to consider his answer, and before he got it out, Solomon stepped back in. With eyes lit up, he said, "Yes! That's exactly what I'd like. I've always heard my parents talk to each other about frameworks and how to think about things, and I've never been able to understand any of it. I want you to show me!"

I turned to Sophie next. "How about you? Would this work for you?" She answered, "Well, sort of. But I like to get advice, too."

I recognized that Sophie wasn't quite ready to let go of her dependence on her parents, so I made a different suggestion. "Well, what if Zac were to ask you to first come up with your own advice for yourself. Then he could offer you a different suggestion so that you could make a choice. Would that be helpful?"

"Oh yes," she responded. "That way he's not telling me what to do, but he's helping me figure it out."

Coaching people in businesses on how to evolve their thinking is an important part of Zac's professional work, and so these suggestions were a natural fit. It just hadn't occurred to him to apply them to child-rearing. After a little consideration, he formed the aim "Make it transparent!" to help him remember the new pattern of engagement he wanted with Solomon and Sophie.

Going Forward: Journal Entries

At the conclusion of the project, I asked participating parents to write a summary in their journals of what they had learned and how it was going to affect their parenting going forward. Here are some of those summaries.

Lily Kellogg Hollister

This goes so far beyond fragmentary parenting models that focus narrowly on developing motor skills, emotional intelligence, etc. It helps me engage with the whole child, my whole self, my whole partner, and potentially the whole world differently. I now see how parents are uniquely positioned to shape the consciousness and beliefs of the next generation, and the implications of employing a developmental approach to this role, which are huge. Parents are in the unique and non-heroic role of evolving and regenerating culture at the hearth. It's a lot of hard work that mostly goes unseen, and it is an important opportunity to grow our capacity to live consciously and creatively, which is essential if we are to raise conscious and creative children.

Rachel Kastner

The process of reflection has allowed me to see my daughter from a more whole perspective and allowed me time to slow down and observe myself. This has enabled me to pause any authoritarian reactions I don't want to have, acknowledge my fears and their influence on my reactions, and consider how I really want to respond. As a result, my relationship with my daughter has developed to a whole new level. I have become more patient and, in general, my daughter has become less aggressive and more responsive. As we work to establish a new rhythm in the way we accomplish tasks, our interactions are becoming more enjoyable.

David Ray

I really thought that being a dad was going to be easy for me, that I was going to just naturally be good at it. But I found myself in a situation that I wasn't prepared for, and it was confusing and overwhelming. At one point I was so discouraged that I was afraid I just couldn't do it. There were days when I actually wondered whether we needed to give this child back.

This project has helped me move past that. It has given me an anchor. Whenever I get overwhelmed, I need to come back to the fact that I'm coming to terms with one particular child, not with all of the ideas other people have about children. When I can do this, I become calm and focused, and it starts to make sense. I can just be with him, and both of us get stronger together.

I no longer expect this job of fathering to be easy. But now I have faith that there's a way—as long as I keep going back to the idea that my boy is being who he is, with his own essence and his own future. Sometimes it's hard for me. I keep forgetting. But that's the way forward for me.

Anastasia Smith

I'm beginning to see that I had previously perceived the parent-child dynamic as child-centric. I'm now seeing that this relationship is continually evolving both child and parent. This requires a lot of inner work and self-realization on my part. As a parent, I must learn to balance my own expression as an individual with what the world expects from me, while creating space for my child to explore her expression of who *she* is.

Additional Insight: Journal Entry

Jessica Handy, who also participated in this project, is the Education Program Lead for Kiss the Ground, a Los Angeles–based education and advocacy group whose overarching mission is "inspiring participation in global regeneration, starting with soil." Jessica expressed deep gratitude for the opportunity to apply her regenerative values to how she raises her children. Here is one of the experiences that she described to me:

My kids participate in a weekly homeschool co-op where we parents take turns cooking the lunches. There are always activities before and after the meal, and typically my kids will say that they are hungry after class. I usually just roll my eyes and say, "You guys should have eaten. There was opportunity to eat and you opted not to." I usually pack a snack because I know what to expect, but I do it with a little irritation and frustration.

I decided to take a different approach one week, and I closely observed my youngest boy, Eli, who is six. At meal time, I watched him grab a plate, sit down, take a couple of bites, and after two minutes jump up to play with his friends.

I called him over and said, "Hey Eli, I just wanted to ask you a question. You know, often after these sessions you tell me that you are hungry as soon as we go to the car. Why do you think that is?"

He thought for a moment and responded, "I usually don't eat my food; I play."

I said, "Yeah, you choose to play during the meal time. Do you think that you are going to be hungry later?"

"Yes," he confirmed.

"What do you think that you could do differently today to prevent yourself from being hungry when we leave?"

"I should probably sit down and eat my food."

"That's a good idea."

He sat down peacefully for maybe another 10 minutes while his friends played. He observed them while taking bites of his food, completed his meal, took his plate to be cleaned, and then went to join them.

I was blown away. I really didn't think he was going to respond in this way. I certainly never imagined that he would follow through and change his own behavior. I saw the power of not telling my kids, "You need to do this, you need to do that," but instead bouncing it back to them and allowing them to reflect on who they are and why things turn out the way they do.

I have been practicing this as much as I can. Though I fall back to my normal ways, I'm grateful to have these tools, and when I'm totally present, being able to utilize them allows for less stressful parenting. I'm becoming a better listener and better observer, and I'm finding ways to create questions that allow my children to make decisions that are going to help them be better people and live regenerative lives.

CHAPTER FIVE

The Regenerative Designer Role

D ESIGN IS FOUNDATIONAL to the manifest world. We are surrounded by the products of design, everywhere from the places we live to the interactions that stimulate our engagement and development at work. We are also surrounded by the results of actions that were badly designed or not designed at all—think of the waste stream flowing into our landfills, for example, or a community that is unprepared when natural disaster strikes. The differences are telling. When something is well designed, we experience a good fit. It works. It looks and feels good. In contrast, when design is neglected or careless, we often end up wondering, "What were they thinking?!"

It's interesting to pause and ask ourselves what design is and why it's important. After all, many of us take our ideas straight into action without pausing to design. Or we simply repeat or extend patterns that were laid down in the past, without thinking about them critically. By contrast, designers are strongly inclined to restrain this impulsiveness, to think ideas through before putting them into motion. This allows them opportunities to ask what the purpose of an action or a product might be and how it might best be achieved. In this way, design has the potential to make contributions that will actually improve the way the world works.

From my perspective, good designers endeavor to build certain characteristics into their designs. First of all, they want to make things workable, attractive, and (in the case of physical objects) manufacturable or (in the case of processes) smoothly accomplishable. For example, if I'm buying a kitchen appliance, I want to know that it will be durable and excellent at the task it's supposed to perform. I also want it to look good and fit with the rest of the things I own (without sacrificing workability—think about how annoying it is to buy something that looks great but breaks down quickly or does a bad job of serving its purpose). In addition, it needs to be designed in such a way that a company can actually build it for me. These functional aspects of a designer's practice generate the baseline that makes it possible for me to build a lasting relationship with a product or service and the company that markets it.

But beyond functionality, designers seek relatability. They want users to feel understood, as if products or services were custom-tailored to their lifestyles. They also want the people who execute their designs, and those who present them to the market, to be inspired by how cool and forward-looking they are. For themselves, designers want to feel that the best of who they are is invested in what they make and that each new design represents a further extension of their capabilities.

Most important of all, good designers promote agency in others. Taken as a whole, designers are profoundly generous with the fruits of their creative efforts. They know that they have succeeded when those whom they wish to serve take ownership of the products of design. When this happens, the work of the designer fades into the background because users have found ways to integrate products into their own lives. In these cases, users lay claim to what has been designed for them because they experience a perfect fit with what they are trying to do. Whether it's an article of clothing that enables the wearer's self-expression or a planning session that generates a new direction for an organization, the emphasis has moved from the designer's creativity to that of the user.

Well-designed processes and objects enable the people who use them to pursue the lives they are seeking to make for themselves, their families, their businesses, and their communities. When users engage with something that has been successfully designed for them, they have no difficulty integrating it as a natural expression of their own creativity.*

The Essence of the Regenerative Designer

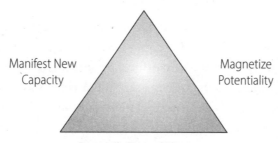

Manifest New
Capacity

Magnetize
Potentiality

Reconcile Toward Elegance

Design is always by someone and for someone. In addition, at a regenerative level, design is concerned with essence and potential. This means that regenerative designers restrain their tendency to do what they are good at (what they already know how to do). Instead, they start from the essence of the users they are designing for, asking themselves, "How can I get in touch with who they really are and what's going on in their lives? What is this event or product that I'm designing supposed to contribute to their lives?"

Contact with the essence of the user generates a strong magnetic pull for a designer. Once the person or group has come to life in a designer's minds, it is no longer conceivable to deliver an off-the-shelf design. The potentiality that exists in the user's life calls forward a similar potentiality in the designer, who will seek to go beyond themselves to create something

---

*I see a significant contrast between regenerative design and the popular notion of *design thinking*. Whereas regenerative design begins from the unique and specific potential of a situation and works to develop the capacity to bring this potential forward, design thinking emphasizes problem solving as a way of arresting disorder. In other words, the two operate at different levels of paradigm.

that is both new and deeply appropriate for the situation. In this way, a designer grows and develops by serving the growth and development of their intended end user. *Magnetize potentiality* is the name I give this process because of the connected, mutually uplifting field that is generated between the one designing and the one for whom the design is made.

I call the regenerative designer's purpose *reconcile toward elegance*. All designers know that the challenge in design comes from juggling competing or even contradictory goals and requirements. From a regenerative perspective, it is important for designers not to engage in trade-offs and compromises with regard to these apparent conflicts. Instead, a regenerative designer seeks to *reconcile* conflicts by shifting to an essence-based view of the dynamics at play. They ask, "What is behind what this client is asking of me? What is truly needed in this situation?" When a designer is able to discern what is really going on and what is most important, the complexities tend to fall away and the elegant solution becomes apparent. The designer's work is to see beyond the horizon of the client, who enthuses, "I would never have known to ask for that!"

Regenerative design serves more than making things work better or making them more beautiful. Its real value lies in *manifesting new capacity* for those who are on the receiving end. This means that a regenerative designer never loses sight of the fact that the larger result they are working toward is the user's evolved capacity for thinking, discernment, and action. By seeing beyond the client's horizons, by understanding the client well enough to know where they are going in their life and what stands in their way, a designer can provide the necessary tools and solutions. But this doesn't yet meet the criterion to expand the client's creative capacity. For this, a regenerative designer needs to bear in mind that whatever they provide should have the effect of increasing the user's autonomy and agency.

Let's say a designer is called on to create a process to help an organization's sales team engage customers in a more caring way. A designer who is working at the do-good level might decide to train the sales team in active listening techniques. Although this might put a few new tools in the salespersons' kits, it won't evolve their capacity for discernment or support independent creative thought. If anything, it will introduce a one-size-fits-all solution that reduces both agency and responsiveness.

Sophisticated customers know when they're being run through a rehearsed routine, and they usually don't like it.

By contrast, a regenerative designer might look at this assignment and realize that what is needed is for every salesperson to learn to approach each customer as an individual with unique aspirations and potential. In other words, members of the sales team need to learn to do good design and thereby engage customers in developmental, one-on-one relationships created specifically for them. Such an approach really would manifest expanded capacity for the sales team, the company, the customers, and even the program designer who had to create it.

Experiencing the Regenerative Designer Role

Sylvia Raskin works as a program designer at The Prosperity Agenda, a national nonprofit that collaborates with partners to offer financial wellness programs based on and honoring the lived experiences of families impacted by poverty. Her designs enable partner organizations to create trusted spaces where community members can talk about money, engage in peer-to-peer learning and support, and celebrate their own financial savviness.

Through her participation in this project, Sylvia made two significant discoveries. First, the qualities she was intuitively attempting to bring into her design could be named and described with precision, making it more likely that her partner organizations could consciously deliver them. Second, she had been so narrowly focused on the experience of program participants that she had failed to see the full transformational potential of her design for partner facilitators and organizations.

Sylvia was aware that creating essence-to-essence connections among participants was important, but without the language to describe it, she was struggling to make this idea understood by her colleagues. Once it was named, she could immediately see the opportunities for *magnetizing potential* across her work: through peer-to-peer relationships among participants, in the dynamics between facilitators and participants, and with regard to how partner organizations saw the roles they could play in the lives of the communities they served.

This led her to recognize a key missing element in her work and allowed her to generate a *reconciling* idea. In her journal, she wrote,

> When nonprofits focus on creating behavioral change among participants, it is easy to become stuck in the Arrest Disorder and Do Good paradigms. Although these organizations operate from a strong set of values, they don't often spend time thinking about shifting their own attitudes, behaviors, and judgments. This can cause nonprofits to overlook the regeneration that is possible when an organization develops an essence-to-essence connection with each client or stakeholder, with the goal of magnetizing potential for both sides of the relationship. Organizations and staff have the potential to adapt, based on what they learn from participants.
>
> I'm beginning to see my program in a three-dimensional way. My clients are nonprofit organizations, and so I have an excellent opportunity to help them move to a regenerative paradigm in terms of *manifesting capacity* in their employees and participants. We can speak directly to the opportunity for nonprofit employees to express their essences in their roles as facilitators and coaches by sharing power and potential with community members. Magnetizing essence-to-essence connections can move across a whole organization to transform the way it thinks about itself and relates to the people it serves.

Finding the Right Level

Jennifer Atlee is based in Montague, Massachusetts. Her company, Atlee Research, works with businesses in the green building industry and other sectors to enable sustainable and regenerative resource flows. During the research project, she was helping to design a governance structure for mindful MATERIALS (mM), a network of building industry practitioners that has created a shared online platform for the purpose of simplifying the selection of building materials that are better for the environment and people.

Jennifer was able to use the levels of paradigm to recognize a significant blind spot in her practice as a designer. As she put it in her journal,

I have this image of designers as catalysts who provide seeds for the transformation of thinking and action, but I've focused on the larger systems that we're seeking to transform, rather than on my own daily practice. From this process, I could suddenly see the usefulness of reflecting on the paradigm I'm actually working from in my day-to-day activities. I started to sense when I was working from a different paradigm than I thought I was, and to approach this observation as an opportunity to grow in practice rather than as a reason to berate myself for not living up to my ideal.

When I design a meeting I can be pretty single-minded, with a lot that I want to get done. But this means that I'm not seeing myself or my colleagues as wholes. As a result, I can actually be operating from the Value Exchange Paradigm with objectives from the Do Good Paradigm.

With regard to designing at a more regenerative level, my breakthrough came from honing in on the magnetic potential between wholes. For example, in the case of mM, I designed a meeting to explore how the organization's structure and purpose statement could become a magnetic attractor to engage purpose-aligned individuals and companies. The conversation reconnected us to the inherent dynamism of mM (a quality that I was concerned was getting lost as the organization went through the formalizing process of setting up governance). I was able to pull this off because I was holding very clear in my own mind the essence-to-essence connection that was possible between this organization and the people it serves, a group that included those on the call.

Applying the Seven First Principles

Laura Weiland is director of the Omega Center for Sustainable Living at the Omega Institute, a holistic education center in the mid-Hudson Valley of New York. Her work bridges community outreach, project management, staff development, and public education, as she attempts to guide the organization toward increasingly effective co-leadership in the regeneration of the Hudson watershed.

Laura often gives tours of her center to a wide variety of groups and visitors. Here is what she wrote in her journal about the effect of her participation in the regenerative life research project on this aspect of her work as a deisnger:

> Our center is housed in an ecological building that includes a natural wastewater purification system. This system treats all of the sewage and gray water from the entire Omega campus by harnessing the life processes of plants and microorganisms.
>
> In the beginning, my tours tended to be fairly rote. Usually they were for the general public, so I wasn't particularly aware of who was with me or what was in their minds. I worked from a script based on stories and information that I'd gathered in order to create a presentation that I thought would be interesting. Most visitors became engaged and asked questions, but I often didn't spend much time thinking about who was there or why. I just gave them the tour.
>
> After I joined the research project, I resolved to design a new approach. An upcoming visit from some college professors offered a good opportunity. At the time, I was bogged down with other work and would have liked to give the tour to someone else to do. But when I reviewed why they were coming, I realized that I would be the best person to talk about curriculum and how we've used our building as a teaching tool. Here was an opportunity to practice and observe myself in the regenerative designer role. My aim was to engage fully and see them as *whole* and unique human beings, rather than as tour participants. For a designer, this question, "What is the whole?" is key.
>
> As we moved through the tour, it was very easy to discern the *nested* systems the professors were embedded in—their own scholarship, their work with students, and their colleges. I couldn't help thinking about systemic relationships within their own institutions and also, *potentially*, with mine.
>
> This led me to notice the emerging excitement among us about what we were each doing. There was an important moment when we shifted from telling each other things to discovering a deeper match among us, our organizations, and our personal passions. When we got to that level of connection, a wonderful creative space opened up; we had generated a *field*. We began to think together about how we could partner and ways for them to participate in our next round of work at Omega, coming up with ideas that fit perfectly with their own *essence* work. Suddenly, I

could see the *nodal* engagement I wanted to have with them. I knew how I could help them grow the ability of their students and themselves to transform the way Omega contributes to its ecosystem—a relationship that would be *developmental* in all directions!

On reflection, I'm fascinated by the regenerative practices of imaging and guiding design by the seven first principles. Through this process, I saw a clear and natural order unfold in my engagement with the professors.

Managing Inner Obstacles

Spencer Sight is an interior designer who creates and manages beautiful spaces for visitors to Kansas City, Missouri. He recently found himself at the center of a local controversy when he undertook the redevelopment of a storied and beloved building that had long functioned as the epicenter of the city's arts scene. Sight reported in his journal that during the transfer of ownership,

…one of the original tenants who had been there for a long time decided to leave and fabricated a story that they had been evicted. This falsehood, coupled with the sale of the building, triggered a collective fear that the area was being gentrified. The story rippled through the community, and I found myself trapped in the defensive posture of damage control. I became terribly concerned with how I was being perceived, investing a ton of attention into trying to recalibrate people's impression of the situation.

When I joined the regenerative life research project, I immediately realized that I was caught in a recurring pattern of energy drains— putting out fires, combating negative opinions, and justifying myself. By recognizing and naming the patterns of *identification, fabrication,* and *waste* I was able to acknowledge my situation and set it aside. This opened my mind to new possibilities, and I was able to step away from the role of firefighter and back into the role of designer, where I belong. I began to focus on the fact that I have created more allies than enemies since the project began and that I can proceed creatively, without worrying about approval. I started finding a more regenerative way to engage with those around me.

I began to listen deeply to what the community desired. I had conversations about what the neighborhood would like to see. It became clear that, in fact, the immediate neighbors were relieved that something new was happening on the property. They saw the coming change as a way to activate this corner of the city, a necessary disruption to initiate a process of regeneration.

While in the past, my arena of design has been interiors, this newfound perspective helped me see an opportunity for social and cultural design. Six months into the project, I have filled the first floor of the building with local retail artists and artisans, helping this neighborhood crystallize into the one and only local retail destination in the city. As I've expanded my definition of who I am as a designer, I've begun the creation of an inn, where visitors can experience a really unique part of town, a place that both locals and tourists can enjoy.

Generating a New Pattern

Ed McGraw is an architect based in Syracuse, New York, where he is cofounder and CEO of Ashley McGraw Architects. At the time of the regenerative life research project, he was overseeing a design team working on infrastructure for a school district. Here's what he reported in his journal about a change in his thinking that generated new patterns in his work with team members:

> There were four small-scale design opportunities whose potential and impact we were trying to optimize. The team included an experienced project manager with whom I have worked for many years, as well as two talented young designers who were given responsibility for design. I consider my project manager to be a linear thinker, an identify-the-problem-and-fix-it kind of person. (This is how many of us were trained in design school.) Because I know him so well, I had already prejudged him, assuming that he would be unable to elevate his thinking.
>
> I was also nervous about possibly making a bad impression on an important client. I wanted the team to use the stakeholder engagement processes and exercises we had developed in the past, because a lot of work had gone into them and they had been somewhat successful in

other situations. The idea of these exercises is to engage client groups in explorations of the meaning of the designs we are developing for them, and at the same time to protect design teams from being pushed to come up with solutions too early in the process. The project was on a short schedule, and I have to admit that I started out trying to exercise too much control over the team. After all, I'm the CEO, right?

But after joining the regenerative life research project, my thinking changed. I introduced the entire team to the Levels of Paradigm Framework, referring to it as levels of thinking and working. I used past projects to illustrate how our work is often about problem solving and over-reliant on best practices. We tried to expand our thinking, wondering how far these four small projects could go in terms of impacting larger systems. The young designers grasped the idea immediately, but my project manager just kept resorting to ways he typically works.

Through journaling and reflection, I became aware of how frustrated I was with the project manager, and I developed an aim to be patient with him. I wanted to try to engage each team member from where they were, rather than from where I was. I resolved to listen and reflect more than talk and direct. I reflected on the idea of a non-heroic approach, thinking over past failures to get others to see things the way I thought they should.

Through all of this, I was moving toward less hierarchical versions of both leadership and design process. I was beginning to worry less about outcomes, allowing others to develop their own ideas around the essences of the projects and the communities we were working in. I could see how fear and attachment kept pulling me into problem solving and doing good. I could see that when I acknowledged these energy drains, allowing them to come and go, space opened for the other team members to participate and find their own experience of essence. Their ideas of essence and wholes then influenced the design work.

It became pretty clear to me that my belief that the project manager was unable to think deeper was hindering my ability to allow him to fully participate and develop. My impatience was based in my own fears, attachments, and subjectivism, and it didn't really have anything to do with his capacity. Once I committed to consciously managing my own attitude, the work flowed smoothly, and he was freed up to participate productively.

Meanwhile, I was delighted by how far the young designers were able to take their exploration of the larger living systems and meaningfully relate them back to small projects within individual school buildings. They came to understand the set of nested living systems—watershed, region, city, neighborhoods, streets, school district, parks, families, and kids—and ultimately the place of the school itself and the role a media center renovation might play. Suddenly we were able to see how even very small projects can be leveraged into multiple impacts.

Going Forward: Journal Entries

Sylvia Raskin
As I think about how to apply what I've learned to future design processes, I've come up with three principles for myself.

- **Think multidimensionally.** Who are all the people who have the opportunity to express their essence through this process and its results?

- **Remove the ego.** The more designers step back, expressing themselves through the framework of the regenerative designer, the more space is created for those who will actually use their designs.

- **Keep in mind the magic of the creative process.** Design is neither linear nor purely analytical. Designers see opportunities to set the stage for others to express their essence. This in turn opens a space for users to explore, contribute to, and even embrace change.

Jennifer Atlee
I'm less focused on the beliefs I *want* to hold and more interested in reflecting on the paradigm I'm *actually* working from in my day-to-day activities. I believe that by growing my awareness and understanding, I'll be able to shift how I work over time. Also, I want to go look at the other roles now (particularly the regenerative educator role), because I sense that these will enrich the way I play my role as a designer.

Laura Weiland

When I'm truly in the flow of this role, I dissolve in the process and can watch and feel myself in a pleasant, calm state. Even though I'm actively engaged, it's clearly not about me. It's as though I'm a conduit to bring things together in a specific way, and I can see potential unfold as I go.

I had a profound experience of this when I hosted the Drawdown Learn Conference. Something clicked in how it all came together. I guided and shaped the event from the stage as well as behind the scenes, and at the end there was a heartfelt standing ovation for me. I knew how important my role was in what was happening, yet at the same time I had the profound sense that none of it had anything to do with me. When a challenge came up, I showed up to help resolve it, but I knew that it wasn't personal to me. Also, when I received affection and praise from the audience, I clearly understood that it was not personal or about me. The source of regenerative design was seeing people in front of me as living wholes and caring deeply about them.

I've become aware of how easily I can get lost in a role at work. This can lead me to fall into the pattern of playing it from a do-good mind-set. I've gotten really clear that unless I bring enough consciousness to see whomever I'm interacting with as unique, I can't step into the power of the designer. So my aim is to remember to see every person as a whole human being, which for me automatically evokes caring, whether I like the person or not. This naturally quiets judgments and fabrication, and it evokes the guidance of the other six principles of regeneration.

Ed McGraw

I've received a lot of value from keeping a journal and using specific questions to help me look at how I'm thinking. "What's really going on here? What is the potential of what is happening?" I've begun to see how my levels of being and thinking can evolve as I care more about the whole and less about self.

Moving forward, I see myself reflecting more on what is driving my interactions with others. I especially need to develop capacity to identify and understand essence. I play a role in the development of the people in our organization, as well as with clients and stakeholders. What capacities will I need to develop in myself in order to be of service to these people and the systems they are nested within?

Additional Insight: Journal Entries

Mario Yanez, another project participant, lives in Brooklyn, New York, where he is the director of Inhabit Earth, a global organization that harnesses whole systems design to cultivate regenerative communities in diverse bioregions. He used the research project to rethink the way he manages time.

> I am gaining a new sense of how to focus my time and energy. Before, it was completely haphazard. I had a general strategy but was constantly waiting for the right energy—interested collaborator, grant deadline, client opportunity—to come along and provide the motivation. This meant that I was enabling the very thing that I feared, fragmentation of my creative energy caused by allowing outside agency to dictate how I spent my time.
>
> I've figured out that I don't need to wait for inspiration or an outside deadline. I can shift the locus of control to an internal space. I've begun to design a daily, weekly, monthly, and seasonal ecosystem to harvest my fluctuating energies, not a static schedule but a dynamic space with various niches that interact with one another synergistically. I have been honing the understanding of myself as designer for some time now, and this gives me a way to call forth the best and highest uses of my creative energies at any given time. I believe many creative people struggle with this issue, and if I am able to find a new way through, it could benefit others as well.

Research participant Bruno Dias is a freelance architect living in Lisbon, Portugal. As part of a current design project, he refitted a robot arm from an auto assembly line with wood-cutting tools in order to shape local cedar logs into precision-cut pieces of furniture art. His designs are based on his investigations into the internal structure of the wood using a microscope.

> This started out as a fairly straightforward woodcraft endeavor. But being part of this research project helped me realize that I was losing much of

the potential of my idea by not adequately honoring the local materials I was using and the place they come from. This refocused me on essence. I started thinking about the essence of the wood, the essence of my project, and the essence of this place. (Searching for the story of this place also led me to get interested in the ancient patterns that prehistoric settlers had imprinted on rocks nearby. These too have been incorporated into my designs.)

Now I've begun to think about how this project can have a beneficial impact on local forestry practices, so that my project will contribute to the vitality and viability of its nested wholes.

CHAPTER SIX

The Regenerative Earth Tender Role

W HEN I WAS SEARCHING for the right name for Earth tender role, I was influenced by Kat Anderson's book, *Tending the Wild*. Anderson describes a seamless integration of humans and natural systems in California before European contact. The indigenous peoples she studied understood that they had important work to do to keep their ecosystems healthy, abundant, diverse, and productive—they were Earth tenders.[1] The definition of *tend* is to "look after, watch over, and care for." In a regenerative context, this means watching over and caring for the inherent potential that resides in and wants to be expressed in every living thing.

Earth tenders share a number of characteristics and behaviors. First, they have a strong interest in how living systems actually work. You might say that they are attuned to life and take instruction from it, and that they are willing and able to find practical applications for the understanding this gives them. They are also deeply and constantly aware that they are embedded in a living world. This is their fundamental orientation, in contrast to the idea of having dominion over Earth and its inhabitants.

Earth tenders willingly take on responsibility for speaking on behalf of life, and they strive to generate or sustain a culture that shows reverence for life. They come from many fields and disciplines—farmers, gardeners, ecologists, foresters, landscape architects, and civil engineers. Often they are people who simply love nature and have developed some of the skills and leanings of naturalists. But along with any specialized knowledge they may have, they also practice a discipline that might be called *indigenous science*, which particularizes rather than generalizes and studies phenomena in context rather than attempting to eliminate variables. This makes them radically attentive to differences and indifferent to averages.

Earth tenders are intimately connected to the ways we secure food, water, and shelter, which makes the role foundational to the formation and sustenance of civil society. Indigenous cultures around the world have always known this and have woven the wisdom of the Earth tender into every aspect of their lives. Modern science has added certain critical details to our understanding of how living systems work, but it has tragically failed to address the cultural ignorance of modern societies when it comes to our participation in a living planet. Thus, the regenerative Earth tender also plays a critical role in reconnecting the modern world to the life processes that sustain it.

The Essence of the Regenerative Earth Tender

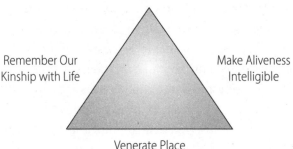

Remember Our
Kinship with Life

Make Aliveness
Intelligible

Venerate Place

The regenerative Earth tender role's core process is to *make aliveness intelligible*. That is, Earth tenders bypass the training that teaches most of us to see living things as static objects, more or less indistinguishable from other objects in their class. Their discipline is to discern and make sense of—to make intelligible—the processes and purposes of living beings.

I like to use the example of animal tracking to illustrate this idea.

Trackers learn to read small signs left by animals as they pass through a landscape. From the relative distance, depth, and orientation between tracks, a tracker can decipher the speed that the animal was moving, the conditions it might have encountered, and the distractions that might have caused it to pause and turn aside from its course. From small numbers of signifiers, good trackers reconstruct in their minds the balletic experience of living and sentient beings moving through space and time.

The regenerative Earth tender role's core purpose is to *venerate place*, holding Earth sacred in both its local and planetary manifestations. Sometimes this shows up as an exceptional depth of attunement to the living dynamics of a place and the development of a systemic understanding of them, similar to the ecological literacy exhibited by indigenous hunters and shamans. Sometimes it shows up as passionate commitment, a willingness to put one's body on the line to protect fellow living beings. Sometimes it shows up in the form of private and public rituals that acknowledge the cycles of life and nature in a particular place. In every instance, the source of these patterns of behavior is reverence for the living world.

The Earth tender role's core value is to *remember kinship with life*. It's easy for regenerative Earth tenders to relate to Earth and all of its creatures because they are family. Indigenous people around the world have always spoken of animals and plants, rocks and rivers, and even celestial bodies as brothers, sisters, mothers, fathers, and ancestors. There is both literal and symbolic truth in this idea. We are expressions of the evolutionary processes of life on our planet, and the material stuff we are made of came from Earth and will return to Earth when we die.

Experiencing their kinship with life causes Earth tenders to show respect for the individuality of living things. It is not a tree that is being cut down; it is a specific tree with a specific history and role to play in its community. It may still be necessary to cut the tree or kill the animal for food or alter the ecosystem through inhabiting it, but as family members, each of these living beings has its own right to exist and to be treated with respect. In addition, Earth tenders cultivate this understanding through teaching and storytelling, helping their communities and youth appreciate the kinship bonds that connect us to nature.

Experiencing the Regenerative Earth Tender Role

Yue "Max" Li is a Chinese conservation research scientist who lives in Tucson and is working to preserve biodiversity in the Sonoran Desert. Early in his education, Max experienced a major insight and recorded with other reflections in his regenerative life journal.

> The biggest threat to biodiversity is not invasive species, but loss of habitat due to human activities. As I started connecting dots between environmental and political problems, I realized that ecological health and social justice go hand in hand.

In this context, he is currently using his training to *make the living processes of a single plant and its environment intelligible.*

> As a field biologist, I've been studying and developing management protocols for an invasive plant, Sahara mustard, on 1.5 million acres of federal land along the Mexican border. This mustard can be very aggressive, but it uses a risky strategy—it germinates a high percentage of its seeds when conditions are good. By contrast, native species germinate only part of their seed, hedging their bets.
>
> Basically, Sahara mustard is like our current economy, big booms followed by big busts. This means that in the long run, it is only a threat where humans give it an unfair advantage, such as building roads that accumulate water on their edges.

When he joined the regenerative life research project, Max had used his findings to develop a management protocol, directing treatment crews to spray areas where there were concentrated populations of the weed. But he worried that his approach was labor and carbon intensive and that it relied on herbicides with unknown, long-term systemic impacts.

> Learning about the Earth tender's essence reminded me that I needed to go back to my observation and understanding of natural patterns. I spent a night camping in the foothills of the Mohawk Mountains and

climbed halfway to the peak the following morning to situate myself in the same frequency as the land around me—that is, to *venerate place.*

Then it dawned on me. The worst populations of Sahara mustard occur along the border wall, due to heavy construction and constant Border Patrol traffic. The Border Patrol regularly drags the complex network of roads that they built along the border, creating disturbance and spreading seeds. Without treatment, the resulting dense population of mustard will eventually spill over to the relatively pristine dunes in the interior.

Clearly I needed to focus on these roads. More important, I needed to ask the Border Patrol to cooperate with us by dragging less in order to create less disturbance. To solve the problem of Sahara mustard, we actually need the agency to change its culture and become a steward instead of a disrupter of border communities. This insight has already borne fruit. I've met with public liaisons from the agency who have expressed their support for an officer education program and a willingness to implement the methods I've suggested for reducing mustard dispersal.

I've also shared my insights with the treatment crew, reminding them that this land used to belong to indigenous people. This desert was their food, their clothing, their spirit, and their way of life. European settlers drove them out, taking part of the land for military training and another part to create an illusion of a humanless wilderness. The border wall adds insult to injury by breaking the laws of wilderness protection.

What I want to achieve through these small talks in a big desert is an awakening, a *reminder of our kinship with life,* as a way to lift up the order needed for our social and spiritual evolution. I want to enable the life-giving energies embedded in each human, the compassion *and* the anger. These energies are contagious, and we can use them to bring the peaceful change we want to see in how we treat both nature and people.

Finding the Right Level

Daimen Hardie is based in New Brunswick, Canada. He is cofounder and executive director of Community Forests International, which works with teams in Canada and Zanzibar to decelerate climate change while building prosperity for deeply affected frontline communities. Here's an example of finding the right level that he recorded in his journal:

> Climate change is a huge complex challenge. In my work I need to build partnerships across diverse interests and cultures, because none of us can solve this massive problem alone. These collaborations can easily be undermined by people's fears, dropping the discussion to a value return level. All of the potential gets lost and nothing really improves fundamentally. I've seen that when I can bring a regenerative mind-set I can elevate the conversation, and this affects not only my own thinking but that of the people around me, too. It doesn't work every time, of course, but when it does, it's really special.
>
> Here's a recent example. We're trying to bring together players throughout the international spice trade to build a new, regenerative, forest-based value web that actively reverses climate change. This involves linking hundreds of small farmers in Zanzibar to global distributors seeking an ethical supply chain.
>
> One of the key collaborators in this project has a tendency to approach everything in terms of scarcity and competition. I found myself becoming increasingly defensive toward this partner until I remembered to start from a regenerative paradigm. I didn't need to operate from their reality, but I did need to make an effort to understand it. I relaxed, became more open to how they were seeing things, and let go of pushing for any specific outcome. We seemed to be engaged in a power play, yet by letting go of a seemingly vital strategic position, we were able to discover a more important opportunity, one that would powerfully stimulate the regenerative interactions we were seeking.
>
> By shifting my own thinking, I brought better ideas to the conversation; I was willing to give more. I was also able to perceive more about my associates, getting closer to the core of where they were coming from. This definitely had the effect of drawing my associate away from a fear-based position and into a much more collaborative frame of mind. I think it allowed this partner to consider larger possibilities once I provided what was needed to address concerns about scarcity and competition. We actually went from spinning our tires to a place where this associate has now invited my team to pitch to their largest investor—a transformation that I would have never expected!

Applying the Seven First Principles

Delfín Montañana is a biologist specializing in the urban application of ecological principles for social development in Mexico City. He works with Isla Urbana to expand rain-harvesting practices in neighborhoods where there is a high level of water precariousness, as a practical strategy to secure their water supply, build local skills and self-reliance, and regenerate a culture of respect for the sacredness of water.

On joining the regenerative life research project, Delfín immediately recognized the relevance of the Earth tender essence to his own work and set out to apply it, along with the seven first principles, to an event he was organizing. Isla Urbana had partnered with a number of other nonprofits to address the needs of La Conchita, an old, traditional neighborhood in the district of Xochimilco, which had been damaged by the 2017 earthquake. With foundation funding, they had installed rainwater harvesting systems in the homes of 80 families. Delfín was tasked with creating a daylong event to celebrate this accomplishment and the deeper cultural values it represented. He explained the event to me as follows:

> It's a beautiful area. It used to be chinampas (gardens built on floating platforms), one of the most productive agricultural systems in the ancient world. Now the lake has been filled and the chinampas replaced by houses. The neighborhood is laced with narrow pedestrian streets and can only be accessed by foot. The local people have a deep sense of belonging to place there, and we held the event in the neighborhood in order to celebrate them where they are. The partner who hosted us also prepared all the food, using ingredients that came from the immediate area.
>
> The event was collaborative and thoughtfully woven together. One organization did a workshop on preparing nutritious salads with local ingredients, and the salads became part of the afternoon feast. Another group led a workshop on using plastic soda bottles to make containers for houseplants. A theatre group presented a marionette play about a child's journey to find the rain spirit and ask him to return to his drought-stricken town. The spirit, it turns out, was offended by the careless way humans behave toward water, and the child promised to dedicate

himself to being a guardian of this precious substance. At the rain spirit's invitation, the audience roared out its agreement to do the same.

In perhaps the loveliest workshop, children were taught to use watercolors to decorate pieces of paper, and to fold these into brilliantly colored origami flowers. They were completely absorbed in this activity, and in the end every family took home some of these flowers of the rain, symbols of the connection that each of us has to the clouds.

Asked to reflect on the role of the seven first principles in his thinking, Delfín observed,

I try to create events that are *whole* at a symbolic level. Everything we do is connected, all facets of a single jewel, all relevant to one another. It's a unified space and we are inside of it, sharing laughter, meanings, and capabilities. We are made whole by being in an event that was made to be a whole.

As for *potential*, when we do one of these community celebrations, we are trying to tap into something that doesn't exist yet and to discover more of what it means to be a community and a society. This one lasted from nine in the morning until six in the evening, and most of the people who came stayed the whole day. That's a pretty good indicator of the quality of what was happening. People found themselves in a collective space of enjoyment, learning, and stimulation, and a window opened into what is possible. By the end of the day, I witnessed an informal dialogue begin to emerge in a variety of casual conversations: "We can learn better ways to make things together. We can learn to be participants in the expression of community and how this brings better conditions for life."

We were also weaving in the elements of the *essence* of the place. We started and ended with food and flowers. Learning how to make a very good salad is not only about improving family nutrition, it's also about connecting to place. For thousands of years, Xochimilco was a settlement built around and on top of water, and so all of Isla Urbana's work with water really resonates here. Water and the symbols of water are central to the lives of the people of La Conchita.

Obviously the work of Isla Urbana is *developmental* at its core. We're addressing functional needs, teaching functional skills, and regenerating the relationship of human beings to water. But I've also begun to think about how to bring a stronger element of human development into the celebrations themselves. How do we make participants conscious of the fact that the aliveness they experience when we are together is something that they have co-created, something that they can bring into daily life in the neighborhood?

For me, *nestedness* is something you feel. The idea of systems is an abstraction, but nestedness is an experience. So I'm trying to figure out how to provide this experience for people in their lives. This is part of the purpose of the puppet theatre piece. Through the story, people can feel how individuals are nested in families and communities, which are nested in a living landscape. Then, at some point, they make the connection to their own lives. They begin to feel their inter-being, and they notice that when they come together, they are an integral part of a greater being that includes them. This starts off being an emotional experience, but my aim is to make it increasingly conscious and explicit.

I feel lucky to be working with water, which I believe is a natural *node*. I encourage people to enter into the water by using it in creative ways, such as painting with it, thinking about it, symbolizing it, becoming one with it. This is why the emotions and experiences are so profound for the people we work with. Water is maybe the most systemic thing in the universe, just by nature of its properties. The topic of water is also nodal in society, in the ecological regeneration of human behavior at a local and planetary level.

When I organize an event, it's clear to me that the *field* we create is an expression of our state of being, which is then picked up and expressed in the event as a whole. Still, this practice of field perceiving and field generating hasn't yet become fully integrated in every aspect of my life. I want to learn how to surround myself with the field that will transform the situations that I'm in. You can't create an event that generates a certain quality of experience if you aren't living that experience yourself. But I know that with enough focused intention, a small event in Xochimilco can create a field of resonance that influences the district, the city of Mexico, and beyond. It's not a question of scale; it's a question of quality.

Managing Inner Obstacles

Philippe Choinière lives in Quebec, where he is a permaculture farmer and the cofounder of Oneka Elements, a maker of carefully crafted and organically sourced personal care products. Some of the herbal extracts used in Oneka products are grown on Philippe's family's certified organic farm. Both Oneka and the farm aim to give back to social and ecological systems by the way they do business. Here is what he recorded in his journal about effects of inner obstacles on his efforts to achieve high-level professional aspirations:

> I am an Earth tender at my core, but to be this Earth tender I have also become an entrepreneur. Without the business that we built, I wouldn't have had the means to take over the family farm from my parents. Also, the farm is limited in its systemic impact, whereas by sharing our business model and sharing our thinking process, we are really leveraging the effect we have in the world. This means that I am also learning to be not only a regenerative Earth tender but also a regenerative educator.
>
> During the research project, I became aware that my *fear* was clearly disconnecting me from the essence of the Earth tender role. I was on Instagram looking at the beautiful pictures of a competing brand and getting more and more jealous and uptight. I caught myself making a plan to post bigger, better pictures just to outcompete them. But this is not the essence of me, our farm, or our business, and it certainly isn't the essence of an Earth tender or educator. It was just me feeling afraid of losing. So I stopped myself. I wasn't able to completely eliminate the fear, but at least I didn't carry out my hostile plan.
>
> On another occasion, I was talking with the owner of this same brand. As she told me how she is now selling in New York and other major markets, I watched the same feelings reappear—*fear, jealousy, envy.* A little voice inside of me started to say, "Well I can do this too, and I'm going to." I had once again become totally disconnected from my essence. But how can I be regenerative if I am spending my time bouncing from one reaction to another? If I am just trying to outcompete, then I am not serving, I am not innovating, and I am not being creative.

Generating a New Pattern

Jessica Handy lives in Los Angeles, where she runs educational programs for Kiss the Ground. She also is a regenerative parent, and as we saw earlier, she participated in that part of the regenerative life research as well. Here is how she reflected on generating a new pattern in her professional life:

As a registered dietitian, I am periodically asked to present and give workshops that focus solely on human health. This poses a challenge for me because, as an Earth tender, I believe and teach that human health is directly connected with planetary health. What we do to our planet, we do to ourselves. Often this is not a belief or an interest that is shared by the client, and this can make me a little shy. I sometimes find myself making generalized assumptions about what clients will find acceptable, and during those times I allow this to shape what I offer them. When I do this, I find myself unable to fully represent what I stand for.

By reflecting on what it really means to be an Earth tender, I was able to observe what I was doing and intentionally alter my approach. I was recently asked to lead a workshop for a wellness event. I used the opportunity to educate and broaden the client's thinking. I posed questions that introduced the idea that wellness goes beyond what we put in our mouths. For example, "What are some of the environmental impacts of our buying and eating decisions? How do these affect our health?"

This opened up the conversation and allowed us to explore areas well outside the narrow invitation the client had originally made to me. The client is now allowing me to assist with sourcing the food for the event and is willing to use reusable plates and silverware. I'll be able to point to these aspects of the day as examples in my workshop, creating a tighter connection between learning and experience. And I'm hoping that this will help the sponsors launch their own journey toward thinking regeneratively and holistically.

Going Forward: Journal Entries

Max Li
I am convinced that to achieve success in conservation, we must shift from community outreach to community empowerment. This means that we need to be humble, and we need to engage with the most marginalized people to affirm their dignity and restore their habitats and health. Happily, there are many groups in my area who are working on this.

Specifically, I plan to participate in an exciting project in my own neighborhood, repurposing an abandoned elementary school into a regenerative urban farm. It's becoming a place where those who are most marginalized in this marginalized neighborhood can feel safe and find a place to heal. As an immigrant and a person of color myself, I hope that my presence as a scientist and an activist will inspire other young people to believe in themselves and take actions to change their community, state, and nation.

I also plan to continue the work of managing invasive plants on federal lands, which will require me to find ways to collaborate with the military, the U.S. Fish and Wildlife Service, and the U.S. Customs and Border Patrol. By maintaining connections with these government agencies, I have the opportunity to influence their thinking and cultures. And as a Buddhist, I will continue to go deeper into my daily meditation, to be mindful of my ego, and to maintain and build the compassion that I will need for this work.

Daimen Hardie

In the future, I want to get better at anticipating how to elevate an interaction so that I can be ready to take it to a higher level, again and again, whenever the opportunity presents itself. This is so much more effective than fixating on worst-case scenarios and spending a lot of energy on contingencies. I've been burned enough times in partnerships to know that I can't expect things to always go well, but I don't want to focus on that. Instead, I want to give equal energy to modeling what it looks like to pursue potential instead of problems, and being ready to support forward movement whenever regenerative pathways open up.

Delfín Montañana

I need to be able to embody the essence of Earth tender and from there develop the capability to generate a purpose. I relate this to the experience of being fully alive. I form a purpose by instinct, but I want to learn to do it explicitly so that it can guide not only my choices but also those of everyone I work with. Channeling the essence of Earth tender helps me avoid my inner obstacles.

I also want to learn to design in ways that will allow deeper potential to emerge. In the events I've created, most of the results are emotional.

They don't go as deep as they could go. For example, the quality of dialogue is relatively undeveloped. We haven't used our events to co-create new and shared understandings. That's my next learning challenge.

Philippe Choinière
The frameworks are helping me to be vigilant and question my motives, allowing me to catch myself and observe the fear that's influencing my thinking. Then I'm able to say, "Right now I'm not regenerating because I'm being fearful." It's not that I need to avoid the feeling, but I need to catch myself and bring myself back to essence. Who are we, what do we serve, what's our path? I don't want to react to people; I want to be inspired by them. I want to more fully live out the essence of Earth tender so that we can serve, regenerate, and have some impact in the world.

Additional Insight: Journal Entry

Ian Johnson, another research participant, lives in Portland, Maine, where he is a senior director for Linnean Solutions, a company that guides local governments, organizations, property owners, and communities in reaching ambitious resilience and sustainability goals. Ian used his participation in the regenerative life research project to take a hard look at how he was approaching a very high-pressure project.

I found myself working on a project for which my team had very little design input. We were expected to produce a high-performing, energy-conserving building after the fact. It was a situation perfectly designed to generate resentment and burnout, and that's where I found myself heading. Initially, I thought, "Since I have so little power in this role, why should I give it more than I have to?" Happily, being exposed to the essence of the Earth tender helped me shift from the doing side of my role to understanding its potential. I began to see how ripples of change can move out from even a tiny scope of work.

I let go of worrying about whether we were going to meet the highest possible energy standards and put my attention on how the team was interacting. I knew that if we could foster optimism and effective communication, it was bound to influence the results we'd be able to produce. By changing my approach, I found that the project began to change. The team felt lighter, and I worked on generating a positive field in our meetings. I had shifted the scope of what I was working on to something more enduring than just this one building. There were many more projects, surrounding cities, communities, and ecosystems that would benefit as team members changed their outlook and approach for years to come.

Going forward, I see my scope expanding far beyond the scope of a contract. My role as an Earth tender is bigger than what I'm paid for. It's also bigger than my personal hiking or gardening practice. I have come to realize how important it is to help shift others' perspectives in their work and lives, to help them become Earth tenders themselves. From someone who never saw himself as an educator, I now see how vital it is to the work I want to do. The degree to which I can awaken positivity and an appreciation for the living world in every team I work with, the greater impact I'll have on the bigger picture.

CHAPTER SEVEN

The Regenerative Citizen Role

A CITIZEN IS A MEMBER of an institution that is designed to serve the greater good and to be governed by its members. Citizenship is specific to the bodies to which we belong—nations, towns, communities service organizations, governing boards, and so on—and its rights and responsibilities are also specific. True citizens commit themselves to forwarding the well-being of the whole, fighting for what they believe in while at the same time honoring the integrity of governing processes over their own partisan preferences and opinions. In other words, a true citizen will not undermine the whole in order to win wealth, power, or favor.

In a democratic society, citizen is a role that every member should be prepared to play. Otherwise, without full participation from members, it is possible for one or another group to advance its aims to the detriment of the integrity of the whole. This is how authoritarian and antidemocratic impulses undermine institutions, degrading the overall health of social and ecological systems. A citizen (in contrast to a partisan) defines patriotism in terms of the ability of the whole to integrate and benefit from all of the differing beliefs and interests that make up a vibrant civil society. This applies as much to the advisory board of a local nonprofit as it does to the halls of national and international governing bodies; depending on the patterns of behavior we uphold, we either strengthen or weaken the practice of democracy.

In addition to defending democratic principles, regenerative citizens commit to shaping the institutions that govern their lives by evolving their own systemic thinking, educating their fellow citizens, and stepping into leadership roles. This requires a willingness to educate themselves about how a given institution is governed. It also requires the humility and discipline to set aside their own agendas and self-interest in order to serve what's best for all.

The Essence of the Regenerative Citizen

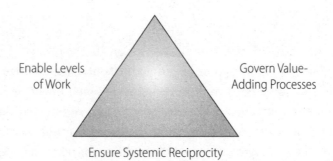

The regenerative citizen role's core process is to *govern value-adding processes*. I use the term *govern* in its sense of directing, restraining, or influencing. *Value-adding processes* (as opposed to value-extracting processes) are defined as ongoing activities specifically designed to generate value for everyone and everything connected to them. As an example, farming is a value-adding process when it generates not only high-quality, nutritious food but also biologically healthy soils and watersheds, viable farms, engaged and knowledgeable farm workers, and vibrant rural communities.

In this case, the regenerative citizen's role is not only to be a farmer in the traditional sense of the word but also to create the systemic infrastructure that encourages value-adding farming, while discouraging value-extracting practices. This is a relatively simple example, but nearly every kind of work, from building a home to organizing an arts festival to running a hospital emergency room, is a process that can be conducted in a value-adding or value-extracting way. The citizen's job is to provide the guardrails that help keep all of these processes moving in directions that evolve a more vital and resilient society.

The role's core purpose is to *ensure systemic reciprocity*. In nature, systemic reciprocity arises from contributions to the health of ecosystems made by their member species, which are in turn sustained by the whole. This is not a transactional exchange, where one individual does a favor for another, who makes a payment in return. Rather, it is participative, more like the love that moves freely within a happy family or the congeniality of a friendly neighborhood café, creating fields that light up not only family members and customers but also everyone who come into contact with them.

One of the indicators of a society's level of systemic reciprocity is its dedication to fostering the personal agency and initiative of all its members, with no exclusions. The work of citizens is to clearly articulate the governing purposes of their institutions in ways that enable everyone to see what is needed and make choices about how to aim their unique contributions in a collective direction. Further, citizens put in place infrastructures that facilitate agency and allow individuals to act effectively on their initiatives. An example is the thinking behind U.S. President John F. Kennedy's mission to put a man on the moon. As a result of this almost impossibly ambitious program, an entire generation was awakened to the importance of math and science in service to national achievement.

The citizen's core value is to *enable levels of work*. In a system as complex as a society, citizens engage not only in different *kinds* of work but also in different natures or *levels* of work. One kind of work, for example, is to keep roads functioning and in good repair. Its next level up is extending or reworking the highway system to meet growing or shifting needs. The level above this is integrating roads into a multimodal transportation system, designed to reimagine the movement of people and goods in an era of planetary change.

At the highest level, a society recognizes that it's not enough to reimagine transportation as a generic system. By moving beyond an all-purpose, improving approach, it avoids giving transportation the power to shape communities (a regrettable mistake made by progressive societies around the world, beginning in the middle of the last century). Instead, it shapes a more life-promoting system based on local conditions, history, and values. For example, for two small Connecticut cities separated by a river, the introduction of water taxis had an immediate, enlivening effect, knitting together two waterfronts that were otherwise isolated from one another. At the regenerative level, a transportation system is designed to be the distinctive expression of a community's unique character and to foster its potential for greater health and vibrancy.

Work must be conducted at all of these levels if a society is to maintain functioning while at the same time preparing for and creating its own destiny and future. All levels of work may be conducted side by side, as they are generally undertaken by a diversity of industries, businesses, and individuals organized around different schedules and locations. However, a society is able to realize its greatest evolutionary potential only when it allows the higher levels of work to inform how it carries out the lower ones. This is why it is important for citizens to become conscious of the nestedness of these different levels and to see their relatedness. Without this consciousness, a community will imagine conflicts between, for example, the immediate need to repair last winter's potholes and the ongoing, long-range planning for total infrastructure overhaul and expansion. These tasks at different levels are only in conflict when we lose sight of the fact that a community is a living whole. The work of a regenerative citizen is to defragment the way people and their institutions understand civic life so that work at all levels can be carried on harmoniously.

Experiencing the Regenerative Citizen Role

Sam Ford is director of cultural intelligence for Tiller Press at Simon & Schuster, a CBS company, and he is an affiliate of MIT's Program in Comparative Media Studies/Writing. He divides his time between New York City, where he is a Knight News Innovation Fellow at Columbia University's Tow Center for Digital Journalism, and Bowling Green, Kentucky. He participated in the regenerative life research project as both a citizen and a media content creator.

One of the things I've discovered is that the theme of polarization—red versus blue or rural versus urban or coastal regions versus middle of the country—only makes sense when you are speaking in broad generalizations at the national level. The minute you get down to the local level, dynamics change dramatically.

For this reason, I wanted to experiment with a localized approach to citizen engagement, and I helped American Assembly at Columbia University set up a project in Bowling Green, Kentucky, that brought together local news outlets, citizen groups, business organizations, and city government. We called it "civic assembly," and it began with a virtual town hall meeting based on Polis, a polling tool that was created for local governments.

For two weeks, the local newspaper posted a broad question for all those who live, work, and spend time in Bowling Green: "What do you think would improve our city?" People submitted their responses, the paper compiled and published them, and then everyone participating had the opportunity to vote *agree, disagree,* or *pass* on each of the written responses.

The newspaper was astonished at the level and intensity of involvement—more than 2,000 people participated during those two weeks. It was a beautiful example of *ensuring systemic reciprocity* by enabling people to engage from their own agency and initiative. Afterward, we helped the assembly analyze and report on the results, and they called an in-person town hall meeting, where several hundred people showed up. They invited various stakeholders to come and present on issues that were raised by the polling.

One of the things that surprised us was that among the hundreds of submitted statements, the vast majority garnered significant popular support. This challenged the widely held belief that Bowling Green is a highly polarized community. Sure, there are hot-button issues over which there is strong disagreement, but mostly we agree. One of the implications of this is that if civic leaders or news organizations always start with hot-button issues, then a perception of polarization is the result. This gets amplified by the media, which tends to consider only those topics around which people are polarized to be newsworthy. The *value-adding processes* that keep a community healthy and moving forward together (such as fair housing and food distribution and safety) are more important and relatively noncontroversial. They really should be the center of our report-age and attention.

City officials were also surprised by the civic assembly results. They noted that it was probably the first time that so many people had come together in the same room to talk about the question of division in our town and our country. Gatherings tend to be organized either for social purposes, such as the retirement of a popular official, or around specific civic projects. These larger conversations are rare and don't draw much participation. This highlighted a gap that officials hadn't noticed; they believed that they had great community visioning processes in place, but civic assembly enabled them to see that we had never actually talked about who we were as a community in any comprehensive way. In other words, they were woken up to a new *level of work* that they could and should be doing with community members.

Finding the Right Level

Kitty Farnham lives in Anchorage, Alaska, where she is a primary orga-nizer for Alaska Catalysts, a volunteer group of community activists. Kitty had been the main source of energy, ideas, and action behind the group from its founding in 2005 until she left in 2011. Recently Alaska Catalysts has reconvened, with the aim to grow a lasting, activated, vibrant network in service to the whole of Alaska. To achieve this, it is clear to Kitty that both she and the group need to evolve beyond their outgrown patterns. She wrote in her journal about identifying the paradigm she normally works from and moving up to the regenerative level.

In the past, Alaska Catalysts wasn't sustainable without my active leader-ship; it went dormant when I had to step away. We had shied away from explicitly converting energy to action, relying instead on the hope that good things would simply happen as a result of networking. We lacked a collective sense of purpose, and we were limited by my own attachments and ideals, my desire to operate within the Do Good Paradigm. Thus, the organization lacked the rich possibilities and essence of the whole of Alaska, and it failed to make good use of the potential that each catalyst could bring. Without the focus that understanding the regenerative citizen essence brings, we had no unifying purpose of systemic reciprocity and no infrastructure for intentionally producing value at each level of work. And it never occurred to us that we should be working on enabling the systemic health of the state's value-adding processes.

I was eager to integrate what I learned about regenerative thinking into the working of the group. The four paradigms were particularly valuable to me, helping me become aware of the mind-set that I and others seemed to be working within. The paradigms gave us the language and fostered the discernment that we needed to do regenerative work, and when from time to time we forgot, they reminded us that we needed to lift ourselves up out of problem solving and doing good.

At a recent event, we had a collective breakthrough. While the group still doesn't have the language for it, I could see us starting to home in on the essence of Alaska, our unique environment and diverse people. We could clearly see the need to help the state advance in a positive way, not just to arrest our current fiscal and governing disorder. We have long had the heart, assets, and opportunity for truly transformative work, and it occurs in more localities than we know. However, our economic, environmental, and social systems are failing to advance these opportunities.

The Alaska Catalyst network is, itself, a nodal intervention, a network of change agents who can bring forth a regenerative future. We know that our work to learn and apply regenerative thinking and practices in small villages, rural hub communities, urban centers, corporations, and governing structures can be a powerful way to transform the whole system.

Applying the Seven First Principles

Ardell Broadbent is a trained mediator and dissertation coach who is living temporarily in Shawnigan Lake, British Columbia. She is also the founder of Politibanter, a game design company that uses play to help improve the quality of political discourse. In her reflections on her participation in the regenerative life research project, she commented specifically on the application of the seven first principles to the set of games she has currently published online.

I'm looking at the United States as a divided nation, a culture in deep trouble. It seems too big for one person to comprehend its nuances, yet that's the *whole* that I'm looking at. The United States is a unique living entity. This means that we can't simply adopt what works for Scandinavia and expect the same results. We are a different mix, more heterogeneous, with a national culture given to optimism and enthusiasm. And, according to the Pew Research Center, we have a greater impulse toward individualism than any other nation.

Greater freedom, enjoyed equitably by all law-abiding citizens, is the *potential* this nation is trying to grow into, however imperfectly. In our history, we've moved in a progressive direction with the end of slavery, the vote for African Americans and women, more respect and protection for children's rights, more humane treatment of prisoners. Still, we struggle to balance freedom for the majority with regulations that protect the weak and vulnerable and allow them a measure of freedom, as well.

The Democratic and Republican parties are like a couple who want a divorce and can't talk to each other anymore, only yell. Maybe this is where *essence* comes in. We need the balance that each perspective brings, and thus we need to respect what is at their hearts. One of my objectives is to bring in recognition of the good ideas coming from the Green and Libertarian parties, adding these to the principles advanced by the two main parties. We can begin to assemble the puzzle pieces into a better understanding of the whole, instead of feeling trapped in our particular ideologies. This is the purpose of my games: to help all parties recognize their shared values and the benefits of each other's perspectives as we navigate a time of intense change, danger, and opportunity.

As I've begun to think about working with games at the regenerative level, as a *developmental* process, I've realized that they're not going to gain widespread attention if I market them in the way I originally planned. Because my purpose is cultural shift, a transformation of our political *field*, I've decided to provide versions of the games for free as downloadable print-and-play products. This gives people a chance to test them before buying and makes them more accessible.

I now envision Politibanter games as part of a civics curriculum in schools that will eventually host an annual national competition with prizes. I believe that this is intervention at a *node* that will allow a growing population of future citizens to face our nation's conflicted past and move us into a unified future. There is a need to gain a wider view, to step aside from business as usual, and take time to consider our national direction. I approach such action with deep concern, knowing that operating from a perspective that is less than regenerative will cause even more suffering in the future.

Managing Inner Obstacles

Johan Clémançon is an educator and community organizer who lives in Valle de Bravo, Mexico, where he is currently employed as the administrative director of Reserva El Peñon, a community located within an ecological reserve. His participation in the regenerative life research project helped him evolve his response to a perceived threat to the core values of the community and the reserve, which had the potential to undermine multiple stakeholder relationships. He found himself able to rein in his autocratic impulse and use the crisis as a teachable moment in citizenship and self-governance. He recorded the story of how he accomplished this in his regenerative life journal.

In the past I would have approached this critical meeting with the intention to influence the thinking of the principal decision makers by making a case justifying my views and offering a path forward. It would have been easy to use the authority of my administrative role to block opposing views and set strong limits and boundaries. In the worst-case scenario, I could have threatened to leave the project. I would have considered the meeting to have had a good outcome if my proposed plan was chosen over other options with minimal adjustments and trade-offs.

Participation in the research project caused me to take a second look. It made me acutely aware of my vulnerability to certain of the inner obstacles. I am now better able to distance myself from my ideas and connect with the essence of my role as citizen, instead of insisting on the conventional prerogatives of an administrative director. I found myself willing to take the risk of going about things differently, reminding myself that deep transformation in the world can only occur when I allow myself to be transformed.

I prepared for the meeting by spending time with the frameworks and identifying the two main inner obstacles that were affecting me. I set an aim to shift and elevate our collective understanding and to remain aware of the energies at work in me and in the group. On my way to the meeting, I had to keep reminding myself that the conversations were not to be about my personal vision and desired outcomes, which was extremely challenging because the outcome mattered so much to me. I did some breathing exercises and invited the essence of the citizen role to guide my steps.

I also devised a little strategy for dealing with my inner obstacles when they eventually, inevitably showed up. I decided to hire myself as the guardian of my own energy and to welcome the obstacles as reminders of my aim.

I had also earlier laid the groundwork for the meeting, in private conversations with the board members and appeals to our collective commitment to serve the project's highest potential. I explicitly asked each of them to help me evolve my understanding, and I was transparent about my ideas on ways to go forward. I also shared my intention to be unattached to my ideas, especially in interactions with the people with whom I had the greatest differences.

During the meeting, I was mindful of the inner obstacles as they manifested, and this helped me avoid reactivity. I could observe myself and even fleetingly observe myself observing myself. I felt detached from the actual content of the conversation, focused instead on the integrity of the container and the effect this had on participants' level of engagement.

The results were extraordinary. The quality of our collective thinking went far beyond anything I'd been able to do on my own. The group expressed strong emotion as they recognized this expansion in their thinking and the deepening intimacy of their relationship with one another. The person who had initially held the strongest opposing view expressed gratitude for the process and for the way his thinking had changed. There was something quite magical about the energy in the room, a sense of renewed trust in our collective work and its relevance beyond the boundaries of the project. All this would have been lost if I had tried to simply push the adoption of my initial ideas.

This experience has caused me to change the way I conceive of my work. My real value goes far beyond articulating sensible ideas and designing effective strategies to achieve regenerative goals. I now see my role as a developer of individual and collective thinking in relation to the purpose and potential of the organization. I always held this as a concept, but now I have a completely different experiential basis for putting it into practice.

Generating a New Pattern

Frith Walker lives in Auckland, New Zealand, where she works for Panuku Development Auckland, an agency charged with regenerating the city's land holdings for the benefit of all citizens. Frith is responsible for the team that works on place making, a concept that can be challenging for some of her colleagues, who are more oriented to the bottom line. She used her participation in the research project to rethink her approach to the creation and presentation of a strategic framework document for the senior leadership team at her agency, and she reflected on the experience in her journal.

In the recent past, my levels of frustration with colleagues who find our work hard to understand or value was becoming problematic. This was draining my energy and impeding my ability to assist my team with their work. The need to constantly find new ways to communicate our value felt disempowering and distracting, and I found myself thinking, "For goodness sake! If you don't recognize the importance of this stuff, I can just leave." I feared that our organization was incredibly close to losing one of its greatest strengths as the result of a narrow, linear project focus.

I experienced a proper lightbulb moment when I encountered the notion of enabling levels of work. I was able to step back and remind myself that all of this, inside and outside of Panuku, with people who get it and people who don't, *is* the work. After all, those in our agency who are charged with building material stuff are under their own sets of pressures and fears, and the work they are doing is just as valuable and necessary as mine. My job at this juncture is to help lift us to a conversation of collaboration rather than proving that one mind-set is better or more valuable than another.

So as I prepared for a presentation to senior leadership about my team's strategy, I told myself, "Walk your own talk and build the love. And do it your way." This meant pictures and stories alongside the graphs and strategy-speak. Rather than defending my work or convincing the perceived "others" of my narrative, I took the opportunity to communicate my enthusiasm for what we do. I expressed gratitude for the various support we get and assurance that we are *all* in the right place at the right time.

The outcome surprised me. There was immediate and genuine affirmation for what I was proposing: instead of pushback or requests for more clarity, I heard strong words of support for the work we have done and the approach we have built. I have no doubt that the fact that I held no fear, resentment, or anxiety during the session played a very big role in assisting this outcome. When it comes to managing my state, I continue to work on paying attention to who I'm being and to remember my commitment to serve the good of the whole from my heart.

Going Forward: Journal Entries

Kitty Farnham

Alaska Catalysts is developing increasing understanding and ease with regard to regenerative frameworks. At our next gathering, we plan to co-create a charter that reflects Alaska's essence and potential, and is fully aligned with the seven first principles. It will reflect our own distinct set of beliefs, philosophy, principles, strategies, and practices. We're looking forward to gaining new clarity about the value-adding processes and infrastructure that Alaska Catalysts can bring forth and that will enable us and the people of our state to engage more effectively in all levels of work. For me personally, I also need to become a regenerative educator, disrupting our habits of problem solving and doing good by widening the awareness and adoption of these regenerative frameworks.

Ardell Broadbent

I've started to see the problems of politics differently and to discern the essence of my work, my unique way of playing the citizen role.

- Core value: manifesting the nation's essence, its potential for both freedom and social order, accountability, and compassion
- Core purpose: elegant reconciliation that shifts orders of potential; resolving paradox (This can happen in our nation. We just don't know how yet.)
- Core process: reconciling one essence to another

Our various political polarities need each other like yin and yang.

Johan Clémançon

For me, the regenerative life project created a practical container in which to consciously experience what becomes possible when I extend beyond the ego mode associated with doing good (especially when it's hiding under the guise of regenerative work). This offers a foundation for me and my colleagues to evolve our practice. Becoming detached from what *seems* to matter allows what *truly* matters to be honored and embraced.

It's particularly striking to me that the self-governing role of citizen (which is directly related to the idea of serving a greater whole) can so easily be used to project one's own idea of what the greater good is and how to achieve it. It's so much more exciting and fulfilling to see this role in terms of the development of our own thinking and capability, so that we can skillfully engage others in coevolving the systems we serve collectively.

Frith Walker

We are capable of great love and creativity, but we have built systems that focus heavily on the economics, the risks, and the pragmatics of living. We've created the wrong infrastructure for a truly enduring relationship with our planet. I am increasingly sure that we need to move back (or forwards) to the time, in our recent or distant pasts, when we knew how to live harmoniously with each other and our environments.

I am inspired and emboldened by the indigenous knowledge keepers of this land (Māori), as well as my own journeying to discover where my bones are from. I think anyone responsible for city making ought to make space to understand what it really means to be connected to place before they lay pen to paper or unleash the earthmoving equipment.

I continue to be surprised at how simple all this seems—coming back to love and connection, and listening to other humans and acknowledging their space. I know our species is at the edge of a precipice, where we will have to change if we hope to secure some kind of future on this planet. The alternative is to barrel ahead and face catastrophic consequences. I am aware of the potential and opportunity of Aoteorea (New Zealand) if we can wake up and take heed. I believe that love is the thing that connects us at our most basic, human level. I think our capacity for rediscovering the things that truly connect us and balancing the conversation between masculine and feminine, logos and eros, and so forth is the making of our successful future here on Earth.

CHAPTER EIGHT

The Regenerative Entrepreneur Role

I HAVE OBSERVED THREE FUNDAMENTAL characteristics in entrepreneurs that explain why this role is nodal with regard to the evolution of our society. As with all of the other roles we are examining here, I think of entrepreneurialism as a way of being in the world, and thus I don't limit it only to people who are starting up businesses. Entrepreneurialism can show up as creative disruption inside a company or in the form of an innovative political campaign or in the creative ways elementary school teachers energize the kids in their classrooms.

First, the regenerative entrepreneur role is a source of innovation, particularly with regard to how we live our material lives. Entrepreneurs see beyond how things are currently working to how they *should* be working, whether in manufacturing, managing information, or providing services. They see the waste in the system, the blind spots, and the missed opportunities. Instead of trying to push the existing system to make incremental changes, the way the rest of us might do, they jump straight to how they believe it should be. This is why we experience them as disruptive, as having broken the track we were moving down. They are laying a new track, rerouting us toward a different future. Every industry and every society evolves through the work of its entrepreneurs.

Second, entrepreneurs have powerful personal agency. They don't need anyone's permission to work on what needs working on. Somehow the challenges they encounter only serve to fuel their motivation. This is core to the role, and we can observe that those who take it on carry this characteristic into every part of their lives.

Finally, I believe that the mentation of entrepreneurs is distinctive. They have fidgety minds that drive them to try to understand the essence of the phenomena they encounter. Possessed of what appears to be a natural discontent, they are always looking for ways to reimagine things, and they never allow themselves to be limited by lack of expertise or experience. If something needs to change, they have confidence that they will discover how to change it. In doing so, they open the door to whole new ways of working and living for others. I believe that this entrepreneurial mental process is the source of the role's seemingly limitless drive toward innovation and agency.

Experiencing the Regenerative Entrepreneur Role

Alexa Pitoulis has been a lifelong entrepreneur, with a strong commitment to building companies that create social benefit. Initially she was motivated by causes, such as providing workplaces for people who had trouble getting jobs—immigrants, former inmates, people without much formal education. In recent years, her thinking has evolved, and she has become interested in the concept of entrepreneurs as change agents, people who can transform society through the way they do business.

Currently, she is building a start-up in Vancouver, Goodly Foods, where she serves as general manager. The company processes surplus produce—vegetables and fruits that would otherwise go to waste. As she puts it, "I work on reframing the narrative around what most people call 'wasted food' into one that views surplus food as a resource." After two years as a start-up, the company is launching full production and growing partnerships with its buyers.

While she was participating in the research project for this book, Alexa was asked to teach a workshop on social entrepreneurship to a group of university business students. Although the professor asked her to fit the workshop into an existing format, the more she thought about it, the more she realized that this would do the students a disservice. Later she observed in her journal,

I really, really wanted to shake up my students' thinking about the role of social entrepreneurship. I wanted to give ideas to consider that they wouldn't find in their textbooks, ideas that would make them slow down their thinking. One example was working to debunk the cliché that enterprises should solve a problem. I told stories about how I don't work on solving problems. Instead, I work with the potentials of particular communities, individuals, and materials.

As I designed the workshop, I was especially motivated by the idea of *manifesting paradigm shift*. For me this means moving beyond doing good to evolving capacity. I was attempting to help these students see the importance of evolving capacity in themselves, their workers, their customers, and other stakeholders. At the same time, I was evolving capacity in me; attempting to teach this concept forced me to get precise about what it means and how it works.

The workshop was deeply motivating for all of us. I asked my students to reflect on the paradigms from which the businesses they interact with are operating. It was eye opening to realize that none of these social enterprises were actually working from a regenerative paradigm. At the same time, I was engaged in a fairly profound reflection on my own business, which set the stage for its next phase: creating a comparable learning experience for its key people. Teaching this workshop gave me plenty of new insight into how we might evolve capacity for our stakeholders.

The Essence of the Regenerative Entrepreneur

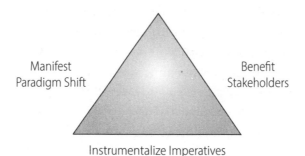

Manifest
Paradigm Shift

Benefit
Stakeholders

Instrumentalize Imperatives

Alexa's story is an interesting demonstration of how a regenerative entrepreneur thinks. Even on a small project like a workshop for business students, she went immediately to work on how to bring new value to them and, by extension, to the school where they were studying. This illustrates her orientation to the regenerative entrepreneur's core process, to *benefit stakeholders*.

A focus on stakeholders is almost second nature to good entrepreneurs. They must learn to simultaneously hold in mind the people who need what they have to offer, the people they'll gather to create it, the material and social resources they'll draw on, and the people who will fund it. Without this ability, they don't stand much chance of starting anything. Assembling a system of key players and figuring out what's in it for each of them is how entrepreneurs do what they do. So it's not surprising that Alexa was particularly focused on helping these aspiring entrepreneurs understand this critical point.

At the same time, Alexa demonstrated the regenerative entrepreneur's core purpose—to *instrumentalize imperatives*. Imperatives in this context refer to the critical social and planetary factors that will ultimately determine our success as a species. A regenerative entrepreneur feels a strong link to one or more of these imperatives and uses it as a basis for creating products and selecting processes. In the case of Alexa's business, there is a strong imperative to translate surplus food (which represents a concentration of embodied energy, water, nutrients, and human effort) into useful products and meaningful work within her community. This, of course, is why she was invited to share her experience in a workshop on social entrepreneurship, where she additionally took on the imperative to wake students up to the real potential and the real challenges of the work they wish to do.

Alexa stated specifically the core value of a regenerative entrepreneur—to *manifest paradigm shift*. Like many people seeking to bring about a more regenerative approach to work and life, Alexa has heard a lot of buzz around the term. Numerous companies and organizations have attempted to repackage their sustainability and social responsibility efforts under the newly fashionable regenerative label. But this only robs the word of its meaning and delays the shift to a new, more demanding, and more systemically beneficial paradigm.

A regenerative entrepreneur who wishes to distinguish the value that they're delivering needs to borrow from the work of educator and media content creator. They need to help their customers, stakeholders, and the public at large understand what it means to shift to a regenerative paradigm. Alexa helped her students accomplish this by making this shift the primary focus of her workshop. She also made a conscious effort to learn from the workshop what she must do to help her own stakeholders make the same shift.

Finding the Right Level

Moira Mills is the founder of Rebl Mom and the Albany pop-up, Adventure Playground, in upstate New York. Rebl Mom provides creative play programs for young boys and offers child-rearing advice to their single mothers. Moira entered the research project for this book with a desire to fundamentally transform her approach to business. But as she told me later, "No matter what I did, I would inevitably end up circling back to an authoritarian or coaching model. I was attached to maintaining my position as an authority figure with my clients, and this was stunting my growth and the growth of my business."

From her position as expert, Moira kept finding herself cycling through the lower levels of paradigm. When times were difficult and she felt threatened, her acknowledged expertise helped ensure that she would continue to generate an income (value return). At other times, her tendency to coach and provide counseling meant that she became the person that moms depended on to help them address behavioral problems before they got out of hand (arrest disorder). At her best, she was aiming to do good for the boys in her program, teaching mothers to make use of the wisdom inherent in their children's patterns of play. But Moira knew that much more was possible, and she found herself powerfully attracted to the idea of a regenerative approach.

Moira's gift for working creatively with the challenges of raising boys led her to start Rebl Mom, but her interactions with the moms in the program were becoming a stumbling block to its development and success.

When she encountered the Levels of Paradigm Framework, it dawned on her that she needed to bring the same open and exploratory Socratic approach to work with her clients that she naturally brought to interactions with kids. As she put it in her journal, "My clients were merely listening to my ideas, rather than taking a journey of self-discovery as active participants. The Regenerate Life Paradigm allowed me to see that my role was to help them connect with themselves."

Suddenly a new world opened up:

I needed to broaden my gaze. Focusing solely on the child wouldn't suffice. I needed to shift my focus to the family as a whole. I needed to work with the whole system.

The way children are raised today robs them of the experiences they desperately need in order to navigate the rest of their lives. I see myself disrupting conventionally held beliefs about children and childhood, and particularly about how to raise boys. But to do this, I need to help single moms build their own capacity for creative nurturance, to tap into their own love of parenting. Obviously, I can't have answers for them; they need to discover their own inner answers.

These insights had an immediate impact as Moira's shift of paradigm led to a shift in her business practices. She has developed a set of inspirational principles that she uses as the basis for engaging mothers in order to stimulate their own creative parenting. More and more single moms have begun to seek her out, and she is now writing a book about her developmental approach, as well as publishing videos and maintaining a website.

Applying the Seven First Principles

Frederik Christian Rasbech is co-owner of the Danish fashion company TWELVEPIECES, which is poised to go from online hobby to straight-up business with collections in physical stores. His partner, Amir Hassan, does design, and Frederik does marketing and operations. Shortly before Frederik joined this research project, the company had a big success at a major fashion fair in Copenhagen, and they knew it was time to launch.

Frederik prepared marketing materials and set up a tour of European stores that he and his partner hoped would represent them. This was something he had never done before, and he was nervous about what he'd created. So before hitting the road, he checked in with his business mentors, who strongly encouraged him to emphasize retail concepts, such as markup and turnover. Unfortunately, the tour didn't get the results he had hoped for.

People liked our clothes and our presentation, but it was hard for us to actually make a sale because our most important asset, our storytelling, was not present in our sales material. This meant that we were perceived as just another clothing brand: we cover your naked body and keep you warm, but fundamentally nothing more.

All of our values were left out. I could easily argue for the potential of our products in terms of economic turnover and beautiful design. But the sales materials didn't make it clear why the buyers should choose our clothes for any reason other than the turnover and the look. It was as though I had forgotten our reason for starting the company, which was to promote cultural diversity, respect, and freedom for everyone regardless of skin color, nationality, gender, and social or economic status.

When he encountered the seven first principles, Frederik found that they helped him break out of the conventional marketing advice he'd been given. By communicating in purely financial terms, he'd failed to introduce prospective clients to the *whole* of his company, and at the same time he had failed to address them as whole people, with interests and motivations that go far beyond profit alone. This bled nearly all of the meaning and *potential* out of the relationship because it turned both sides into faceless, money-making entities rather than finding connections based on distinctiveness and *essence*.

Frederik also had an aha moment when he realized that he had been thinking of his company as a closed system, engaged in purely transactional exchanges with other businesses. This led him to reconceptualize it as *nested* within a larger system that encompasses all of his stakeholders, including his suppliers, distributors, and customers. In this system, he observed, "It's not about products changing hands in return for money; it's about creating a channel for promoting changes in values in return or in service of a more inspired, enlightened, and unified future." Thus, his job is as much to provide inspiration and awareness as it is to provide clothing.

Frederik has taken this *developmental* orientation to the market, and he has also applied it to working on himself. "I have become more able to solve potential challenges in a way that is not about fixing but more about learning and understanding," he reported. By reflecting on his own inner obstacles, he has been able to transform his attitude toward his business partner, which has improved their working relationship and released energy for increasing their collective productivity. He has also transformed his thinking about sales. He no longer focuses on physical products and signing contracts. Now his aim is to communicate the genuine value that arises from the soul and spirit of all the people involved in his business and their dedication to changing society through their work.

Managing Inner Obstacles

Stephen Tracy is a social entrepreneur and cofounder of Keap, a B Corp located in Brooklyn that makes waste-free, nontoxic candles. He has a vision of business as a way to restore the connection between humanity and nature, but he often finds it difficult to maintain this perspective while down in the weeds of day-to-day operations. From his perspective, it's all too easy to end up in the Value Return Paradigm, engaging customers, suppliers, and employees on a purely transactional level. This is precisely the opposite of what he intended when he started his company.

Stephen made a point of identifying the inner obstacles that were undermining his ability to bring a regenerative approach to his work, but the problem seemed big to him and hard to break apart. Here is a journal entry he made during his participation in the research project:

> I started my day feeling positive and connected to my sense of purpose. But then I had to deal with a major supply delay issue, and I ended up feeling stressed and exhausted by all the emails I had to send—some to hound suppliers and others to apologize to customers. I couldn't figure out a way to turn this situation into something regenerative rather than transactional.

It was clearly wasteful. I was losing energy over things out of my control. And I could see my attachments to how things ought to be, as opposed to accepting how they were. Part of being an entrepreneur seems to be dealing with all the many things that take you away from the essence of your work.

Stephen clearly lays out the self-defeating patterns that many entrepreneurs struggle with. Probably the most important is his *identification* with the myth of entrepreneur as superhero, the tireless leader who solves all problems and intervenes personally to place his stamp on every aspect of the business. On top of this, Stephen faces the additional burden of his *attachment* to an ideal of the perfect purposeful company, which prevents him from seeing and working with the potential inherent in the company he actually has.

Halfway through his time in the research project, Stephen had an important realization. His journal continues,

I saw two key patterns that were holding me back: First, too often, I was trying to be the hero in my work situations. I needed to allow myself to be non-heroic and trust others to support me. Second, I was trying to solve everything at once, rather than working progressively by making an improvement and then using that first improvement as a platform from which to make a second improvement—and so on. These two issues were at the root of my frustration. I kept putting everything on my own back; it made me feel important but also overwhelmed. I was buying into all of the clichés about entrepreneurs.

I also kept passing judgment on my daily work and accomplishments, as though everything I did had to be a perfect example of my ultimate ideal. No wonder I end up feeling stressed. It makes much more sense to look at specific arenas and activities in order to identify ways that they could become more regenerative. Then we could develop ourselves to be able to practice these approaches. On a daily basis, I need to put my attention on developing myself and others so that in time we can fully live up to our broader intention.

I was surprised at how simple these ideas were, yet how they opened up my mind. I saw that our development could be a collective learning process rather than a heroic struggle. I could turn daily tasks into moments for regenerative reflection and behavior—not solutions so much as steps toward a new way of thinking and working. To do this I will need to transform my interactions with my own team. I'll need to monitor and journal about my tendency to be heroic, finding ways to rein it in. And I'll need to allow the team to support me so that their own essences can find a space to be expressed.

Generating a New Pattern

Sidney Cano, a serial entrepreneur based in Mexico City and Guadalajara, has teamed with her father to create Duit, a holding company that invests in other Mexican entrepreneurs. Together they have decided to apply what they are learning about regenerative entrepreneurship to these investments. As a participant in this research project, Sidney explored the meaning of regenerative work and what it would require of her. She looked at how she was currently working, where her obstacles typically showed up, and how she might create a new pattern for herself.

Sidney is a millennial, and like many in her generation, she is both ambitious and aspirational. She was raised in a family of entrepreneurs. Her father was a successful businessman in Guadalajara, and some of her siblings have started businesses of their own. Sidney shares with her father a strong belief that business should be a means to raise society up and grow healthy families and communities. These days, she talks about her commitment to creating a regenerative economy for Mexico, an "economy for life," as she describes it.

A few years ago, Sidney agreed to take on the management of Duit. The company is designed to cultivate a business ecosystem, establishing reciprocally beneficial relationships among diverse but potentially complementary businesses. It pursues a variety of strategies, including direct investment, partnership, and the launch of new ventures. The approach is fairly systemic, but as Sidney freely acknowledges, it mostly operates within the lower paradigms. She wrote in her journal,

I grew up learning how to survive in a business world that operated like a shark tank. As often as not, this is the business culture I face where I work. Yet at the same time, I was trying to figure out how to actually add value by making every business opportunity both as viable and holistic as possible. By holistic, I mean that we could gain not only profit but also social and environmental benefits—we could *do good*.

In the last couple of years, my father and I, along with some of the CEOs in the group, decided to work on changing old, toxic practices within the business. For a couple of the groups, we got rid of the weekly report meetings. Instead, we instituted a space were we would come together to think creatively about specific situations, products, or processes that we wanted to improve. I made a point of being a participant in these meetings, not a leader.

Shortly after I joined this research project, I found myself in one of these meetings. I was trying hard to keep in mind the regenerative entrepreneur essence and to channel my own creative energies toward ways to benefit all of the business's stakeholders. But it wasn't working; I felt stuck. My mind kept getting wrapped up in reading the patterns behind what was currently going on. I was so absorbed in helping the team solve whatever they were dealing with, I wasn't able to get up to a level where I could help them create an entirely new pattern.

On later reflection, I realized that I had become much too identified with the role of the hero, the smart businesswoman who can solve the problems and make things work. I had intended to come in as an equal participant, but really I was encouraging my colleagues to rely on me for answers. Also, at a deeper level, I was fearful that if I didn't help them fix problems, our investments might be at risk.

When I spoke to Carol about my experience, she encouraged me to have a look at the role of the regenerative educator. What would it mean for me as an entrepreneur to shift into a role where I was developing the people in my organization, instead of giving orders or solving problems? This felt like a breakthrough for me. I have an undergraduate degree in education, and I was inspired by the prospect of bringing this expertise into my work in business. I needed to figure out how to move the members of the team from being problem solvers who were meeting to work through lists of action items to participants who were engaged in a developmental process. This would enable us to grow our individual and collective intelligence in order to disrupt and evolve the business field we work in.

The next time the team got together, I was prepared. I had spent a couple of quiet hours really thinking about the meeting and what it would take for me to step into the regenerative educator role. Instead of problem solving, I wanted to help people develop the capabilities needed to read the patterns behind the problems, and then move up to a genuinely creative response. In other words, I wanted us to learn how to shift our paradigm.

So I asked them challenging questions to find out what was behind the issues they were facing. I kept pushing to get at what was really going on with both our clients and the systems they were immersed in. It was almost funny to see the surprise on people's faces. "What is she asking us? And why does she keep piling on questions instead of helping with answers?" I explained that I thought we would have better results if we learned how to think together and if we put our attention not just on ourselves but on how to actually improve communities in Mexico.

Since then, it has been amazing to watch how the level of energy just magically rises when an entire group of people shifts from value return to a higher-level paradigm. Everywhere I look now I see the importance of education for entrepreneurial businesses. In one of our partnerships, we've begun to work with interested employees to help them become resources inside the company, so that they can accelerate change. Even more than that, I see the need for businesses to educate their industries and their markets to what is needed and possible if we're going to leave the world better than we found it.

Going Forward: Journal entries

Alexa Pitoulis

I think what surprised me most about this research project was how useful a commitment to regular reflection turned out to be. I was also surprised by how challenging it sometimes felt to actually sit down and start doing the reflecting. Life is busy when you're running a start-up business while raising kids, so it was helpful to have an extra bit of motivation to set aside the time. Reflecting on how I am working, and even more on how inner obstacles get in my way, has been amazingly helpful for focusing and motivating me. Once I can get myself started, I always end up feeling grounded and energized.

Frederik Christian Rasbech

I realized that I had been hiding behind my brand instead of striving to be an inspiring example. So I've committed to being more honest and transparent in conveying my own values and beliefs into how we communicate as a company. This has helped me to connect myself more personally to my work, and it has also shown me how I can change society through my company. I'm learning to communicate and sell our genuine value.

I intend to continue keeping a journal as a practical tool for tracking my process and offering myself a space for reflection. I am also taking forward a newfound awareness of, and confidence in, who I am both personally and professionally. Last but not least, I am taking forward a new way of defining value that allows me to run my company in an honest and meaningful way.

Stephen Tracy

Overall, my greatest challenge is to maintain a regenerative mind-set in my day-to-day activities. It's so easy to shift back to the transactional Value Return Paradigm. Since the research project, I feel better equipped to stay at the regenerative level. My tools are awareness of the paradigms, daily reflection, journaling, remembering to be non-heroic, and allowing myself to work on my core purpose through small, meaningful steps.

It's apparent to me that when I'm writing and reflecting regularly, my ability to manage my heroic tendencies is pretty high. On other days, it is less so, and the Big Goal feels scary and unattainable again. It's a good reminder for me to stick firmly to daily writing and reflecting in the moment. I'm optimistic and excited to continue the journey.

Sidney Cano

I've been trying to live up to what I can currently understand about how to be a regenerative entrepreneur because I can see so much potential value in it. I see so much possibility, not only for my own company but for all of the companies we influence through how we partner and invest.

I recognize that this requires personal work for me. Right now I'm focused on two things. First is the way I prepare myself for team meetings—the consideration I give to my role, the kind of development the group is going to need, and the kind of questions and process that will help them get there. I've also been taking a good look at how I engage people who are bringing in potential business ventures. In the past I thought of these as opportunities to go after (or reject), whereas now I see them as potential developmental relationships. What's important is the contribution that I can make to the success of their thinking and approach. The business opportunity is more of a by-product than my primary goal.

Additional Insight: Journal Entries

Project participant Andreas Wolf is a partner and project manager at Silent Events, a company based in Copenhagen that stages concerts and other events. When he entered the regenerative life research project, he was taken aback by my statement that regenerative entrepreneurs use personal agency for the benefit of *all* of their stakeholders. He said, "The stakeholders I work for are the participants in my events. Normally, I don't see them again after an afternoon or evening. How am I supposed to deepen my work and see the fruits of my efforts?" Then it struck him: "There is actually a whole network of collaborators around me, but I have always unconsciously approached them from a place of 'more for you is less for me.'"

Andreas sat down and mapped out the many collaborators that he depends on to do his work, and he immediately encountered a new issue.

> I became aware that I feel little affection for many of these people and even carry grudges and prejudices toward some of them. This can't be healthy for any of us, and I'm sure it's not good for the business either. But I don't know how to shift the inner blocks that I'm experiencing, especially since they seem different in each case!

From his work in the research project, Andreas learned that he suffered from several inner obstacles. For example, he would fabricate ideas about other people's thoughts and motivations. Or, he was too attached to his sense of his own importance. In some cases, self-absorption prevented him from seeing things from the other person's point of view.

He decided to address these issues head on by taking active steps to improve each working relationship. He set an aim for himself: "Find ways to benefit all of my stakeholders." This is what he had to say about the result:

In one case, all I had to do was realize that the resentments I hold seem ridiculous compared to how awesome this person actually is—sending a short message expressing my gratitude opened my heart again. The next person I invited for a beer; I knew that this would mean the world to him, and I actually enjoy his company when we're not in a professional setting. A third person is a mystery to me; we're on such different wavelengths. So instead of letting this be a problem, I've become actively curious about this person and look forward to "tuning in" the next time we meet.

I even extended this approach to collaborators that I've never met. Without the manufacturer of my sound equipment, I couldn't do what I do, but dealing with audio gear is a major hassle, especially when things go wrong. So it was a breakthrough for me to imagine that I could reach out to them and express my appreciation for the contribution they make to my business. When the sales representative from their factory in China sent me season's greetings, I immediately wrote back to her with pictures of this year's events. She was surprised and delighted, and I find that I'm looking forward to working with her in the new year.

These were good first steps because I now feel connected to my collaborators. But I still have a long way to go to understand what they're attempting to create with their lives. That's when I'll really be able to benefit them.

Sarah Kerstin Gross, another project participant, describes herself as owner and educator at C&K Community Kitchen, a food business incubator in Westport, Connecticut. For many years, she was a major caterer and event planner in New York City. The new business gives fellow entrepreneurs the opportunity to develop and bring their products to market by providing affordable space, education, and community support, including shared marketing and networking. She describes it this way:

My business of the last thirty-five years was based on the yogic principles of focus (*chitta*) and expansion (*prana*). I have always believed that the more detailed and specific I was in planning an event, the more freedom and creativity my clients and staff would experience. Those who took the time to appreciate the precision behind what we were doing gave me an opportunity to teach the foundation on which the success of the business was based.

As a result of the regenerative life research project, I am feeling this essential quality in a new way—that precision *evokes* creative expansion. I have become even more precise in my thinking about what I do, and I can see that underneath all my iterations as an entrepreneur over the years, I have really been an educator and a midwife. I'm beginning to think that when we take on any of the roles of a regenerative life, we become educators. At our community kitchen, we all end up teaching each other and—through our shared organic, non-GMO, gluten-free platform—teaching our customers healthier, more sustainable ways of eating. As people living regenerative lives, we are creating products for the world we want to help evolve, and we are doing so far more effectively as a team than any of us could do on our own.

CHAPTER NINE

The Regenerative Economic Shaper Role

ECONOMIC SHAPERS are people, associations, or institutions that seek to influence the way an economy is working by influencing its governing rules and practices. Sometimes they play this role from within the system by lobbying policy makers or publishing articles in business journals. Other times, they simply ignore conventional practice to invent entirely new economic models, such as crowd-sourcing schemes to help immigrant communities achieve home ownership. A business can play an important role as an economic shaper when it evolves new product offerings that shift the expectations of the market and therefore the responses of its industry. Investors shape economies by means of the expectations they hold; for example, one of the ways that impact investors achieve influence is by redefining the very meaning of *return*.

One of the key instruments that economic shapers use is discourse. Economic theories end up structuring every aspect of our lives, selecting and then monitoring which indicators will be used to describe economic and social health. These are then echoed and repeated in education, political dialogue, and media. The shape of an economy is strongly determined by the paradigms adopted by those who do the shaping. Because economies are pervasive—with big impact on every aspect of life in communities, states, nations, and around the globe—it is particularly imperative that we examine the premises and paradigms that undergird them.

The Essence of the Regenerative Economic Shaper

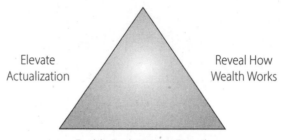

Elevate
Actualization

Reveal How
Wealth Works

Enable Evolutionary Growth

The regenerative economic shaper role's core process, *reveal how wealth works*, refers to the pressing need to make economic system dynamics transparent so that people can consciously participate in wealth generation. Currently these dynamics are opaque, confusing, and contested, and thus it's small wonder most people throw up their hands in bafflement. Even sophisticated investors rely heavily on accountants, lawyers, financial advisors, federal agencies, and other experts to make sense of the byzantine complication of a modern economy. The heavy emphasis on financial capital obscures the real nature of wealth, which includes a host of other capitals, including health, education, and clean water. This oversimplification can severely undermine the wealth and wealth-generating capacity of a community or nation, a fact that is becoming increasingly apparent and that regenerative economic shapers must help us address.

The role's core purpose, *enable evolutionary growth*, underscores the difference between expansion and evolution as ways of pursuing economic growth. An expansion model is about making and doing *more*; it is quantitative and measured by quantifying indicators, including gross domestic product, a calculation that fails to take into account the relative value and actual impacts of economic activity. An evolution model, on the other hand, is qualitative and based on disruptive innovation. It encourages us to displace and replace our current material orientation with practices that evolve the vitality of human beings and the planet. This depends on the development of human creative intelligence, which is the wellspring of systemic wealth. An evolutionary approach to economic growth is grounded in the commitment to grow the regenerative thinking capabilities of every member of society.

The economic shaper role's core value, *elevate actualization*, refers to the need to raise the floor for participation in the economy. Throughout the world, this is currently at the level of the self-defeating and self-reinforcing condition of poverty. From a regenerative perspective, this is the wrong base from which to build a robust and vibrant economy. To solve poverty, we need to shift our attention from the problem to the potential, which is human agency.

A regenerative economic shaper starts from the premise that everyone is born with the capacity for personal agency, which for the most part is neglected or discouraged in the educational and financial cultures of our time and place. What is needed now is an infrastructure that nurtures in people—especially young people—the necessary ability to exercise agency in order to make their unique contributions toward a better-working world. Just as we invest in social security, human welfare, and early childhood development, we need to invest in an agency-fostering platform that allows people to enter adulthood as drivers of a vital economy.

Experiencing the Regenerative Economic Shaper Role

Gregory Landua is based in Great Barrington, Massachusetts, where he is an entrepreneur, an ecological designer, and the cofounder and chief regeneration officer of Regen Network, an international organization with both for-profit and nonprofit arms. The network seeks to realign the economics of agriculture through the use of blockchain services and cryptocurrency technologies.

At the time Gregory was enrolled in the regenerative life research project, he was asked to present at a United Nations Development Program conference in Istanbul on the topic of regenerating and managing the world's ecological commons. He used the regenerative economic shaper essence and the Levels of Paradigm Framework to help create his presentation. He knew that if he was going to create conditions leading to *elevated actualization* for the countless small enterprises that make up the world's agricultural economies, then he was going to need to change the way he engaged his audience. Here are some notes from his journal:

> The economic development community operates from a set of automatic assumptions with a corresponding vocabulary. The easiest thing would have been to adopt this vocabulary, talking about ecosystem services as a form of externalized value with opportunities for "price discovery." But this just represents another way to privatize the ecological commons, an outcome that would be incompatible with a regenerative approach. I might have created new work opportunities for my company, but they would have been defined from within the neo-liberal (value return and arrest disorder) perspective.
>
> As the conference unfolded, I reflected on the essence of the regenerative economic shaper role as a way to understand what was missing in how people were speaking and thinking. It became clear to me that the growth in capacity needed by myself, this audience, and the larger economic development community could not be achieved through a presentation, however eloquent, fact-based, or bold and disruptive it might be. Instead, we would need to experience together an unveiling and reevaluation or regeneration of the foundations of economics—a radical exploration of our discipline based on *how wealth really works*.
>
> I also could see that to pursue such an inquiry with this particular audience, I would need to find creative ways to visualize patterns and principles of living systems. People are working with mechanical mental models that are so all-pervasive there is almost no room for anything else in their minds. What if, through a visualization of biological and ecological systems, we could catalyze engagement with a series of open-ended questions to allow for exploration beyond the habituated mind? Could I begin to introduce the idea of *enabling evolutionary growth*?
>
> Needless to say, given the protocols and tight schedule of a United Nations conference, I wasn't able to initiate an ongoing process of deep

questioning. What I was able to do was offer some disruptions to their current way of thinking and invoke the potential of such a collective exploration. And now I know what I want to work on the next time I'm invited to speak at a major event.

Finding the Right Level

Will Szal, an economist who lives in western Massachusetts, is a Regen Network staff member and president of its board of directors. In the months prior to his participation in the regenerative life research project, he had been working on a new set of legal documents for the organization, including a shareholder agreement for its for-profit arm. He wrote in his journal,

> We were starting to sell equity, and as an entity in service to ecological health, we had some concerns about the ways in which a conventional interpretation of fiduciary duty might compromise our mission. So we began with a statement of ecological responsibility as a basis for developing a new interpretation. After all, our investors are attracted to us because they are as interested in the future of the living planet as they are in financial return.
>
> Before I was exposed to the regenerative life frameworks, I saw my role as builder of the firewall between shareholder supremacy and our company's mission. I was unconsciously envisioning a polarity between us and our investors. I now see how our stockholder agreement can actually invite investors to discern between modes of wealth generation in a way that builds their will to participate more fully in our regenerative mission. In other words, I managed to shift myself from an arrest disorder to a developmental and regenerative approach.
>
> Regen Network has just entered a technology accelerator program hosted by Techstars and The Nature Conservancy. We have come to a verbal agreement regarding the investment terms and will be translating this agreement to legally binding notes in the coming weeks. This will be our first opportunity to put our new stockholder agreement into practice. As a result of working with the regenerative frameworks, I see

this engagement not as a negotiation, but as an opportunity for all parties to further develop our capacities to hold a higher-order understanding of corporate governance.

Applying the Seven First Principles

Bob Mang lives in Santa Fe, New Mexico, where he has spent many years working in finance, property development, and community activism. After retirement, he took on the major project of helping to create a state-based public bank, whose purpose is to grow local economic potential. This is how he describes the project in his journal:

> A public bank will redirect billions of dollars of state funds—which are currently invested in financing large corporations nationwide and internationally—to sorely needed investment within New Mexico. Such a bank will make loans directly to state initiatives, counties, cities, and public school districts, all of which currently rely on bonds for financing their infrastructure needs. This will save bond origination and underwriting fees, as well as interest payments, which in most cases add up to 40 or 50 percent more than the original loan amount. Also, replacing bonds with public bank loans will redirect fees and interest payments away from Wall Street investors and back to the state. This will result in use of the same tax revenues multiple times, enabling substantial increases in investments in economic development and infrastructure without increasing taxes.
>
> In addition, a New Mexico public bank could partner with local community banks and credit unions, leveraging their efforts and securing their viability. The presence of a larger partner would lower the threats that currently endanger their much-needed presence in small communities, for example by reducing the cost of complying with Federal cybersecurity and money-laundering regulations.

When asked to elucidate how the Seven First Principles of Regeneration related to this idea, Bob responded,

New Mexico has enormous untapped *potential* for locally generated economic development, if we can think about the state in terms of *nested* value-adding systems and processes. We live at a crossroads of multiple ecosystems and cultures, which come together to form a unique living *whole*, one whose distinctive *essence* has attracted seekers and innovators for generations.

. *Developing* our internal resources—residents, cultural traditions, and natural attributes—is the most reliable way to grow healthy, equitable, and resilient communities. This is in stark contrast to the conventional economic development approach that the state has tended to favor, importing large, non-locally owned businesses along with new people to fill the jobs they bring. I believe that instead we should make a *nodal* intervention by making value-adding, supply-chain connections between businesses in small, rural communities and those in larger urban areas. Re-localizing supply has enormous potential to generate a *field* of economic vitality and viability for the state as a whole. This approach offers the further advantage of nurturing and retaining our young people, whose innovations will be critical to our economic, social, and ecological future.

Managing Inner Obstacles

Amanda Pinelli divides her time between New York City and Boulder, Colorado. She is cofounder and managing director of CYCLEffect Regenerative Ventures, a venture capital fund organized as a cooperative, with a mission to invest in and grow circular and regenerative economies.

While she was participating in the regenerative life research project, Amanda found herself in conflict with the company's other creator, and she observed in her journal that this was having a profound effect on the work of the cooperative and its members. The concept of inner obstacles became particularly helpful as she strengthened her focus on the cooperative's potential in order to shift the dynamic.

My cofounder and I agreed to enter into several weeks of facilitated clearing. During this time, I determined to set aside my personal attachment to outcomes and instead to focus purely on the possible outcomes that would best serve the collective group. Instead of seeing this conflict as a problem, I held fully present in my mind the idea that this clearing was part of an evolution and an opportunity for the cooperative.

It wasn't always easy. At times I could feel myself trapped in my *identification* with the cooperative's past and the central role I played in its creation. But as I gradually relaxed this sense of merged identity, all kinds of new ideas started to flow. Eventually we came to the realization that we could attract new members who would contribute to CYCLEffect's specific needs. This started us down the path toward developing an evolved version of the organization, one better suited for its current revenue model.

Generating a New Pattern

Ricardo Peón is based in Malinalco, Mexico, where he is working to translate his deep experience in international banking into new models for regenerative finance. He originally studied oceanography, which gave him deep insight into the natural world. He then went on to pursue a successful career in the financial industry, but over time he began to feel a strong inner prompting to step out of this high-speed world. He took some time to reflect on the impacts the finance industry was having on people and the planet, and it became clear that he wasn't interested in merely shifting investments to less destructive or green activities. Instead, he wanted to gain new insight into the inner processes of investment in order to discover their potential for regenerating living systems. In his journal he described his shift this way:

> Initially, I wanted to drop out of finance entirely. Yet I gradually realized that the people I admired the most, the ones doing deeply meaningful work, had very little knowledge of the financial world. To be able to help them, I set out to unite these seemingly opposed aspects of myself.
>
> At the time of the regenerative life research, I was working on several projects, including how to think about a global investment strategy to reverse climate change. My first thought had to do with the increased risks that climate change introduces and the ways these risks are

inadequately accounted for in existing assessment metrics. By including carbon pollution and sequestration in the ways we measure value at risk, I was hoping to link investments with climate change. But although I was using a new concept, I was still operating within the same linear logic that currently governs financial thinking. I needed to go back to the drawing board.

Encountering the concept of the regenerative economic shaper role and the essence triad that underlies it helped to reignite my will. I immediately saw that I hadn't gone deep enough and that I needed to map my understanding of the financial system as a whole from a living systems perspective. I began to see that the way entropy works in nature is similar to how inflation works in the human sphere. Life operates creating order, or negative entropy, in the time dimension. We humans create inflation in our economic systems under the paradigm of debt (the time value of money). In nature, wealth creation needs to be greater than entropy, and human economies only work when wealth creation exceeds inflation. It's a useful comparison, but the debt paradigm may also explain why, in the existing financial system, quantitative growth is favored over the growth of complexity.

This mapping has forced me to expand my thinking. It allowed me to step back and realize that I was working from too narrow a vision of the system. I could actually watch my mind as it tried to shake itself loose from linear and dualistic thinking in favor of a more whole perspective. This encouraged me to go further, to introduce new elements and see how they fit. For example, how do we shift the mind-set by which companies try to reinvest earnings into unlimited growth? What if reinvestment were channeled into a *system* of companies instead of a single, particular one, thereby encouraging the growth of complexity? I can begin to see the implications for a new investment model, and I'm looking forward to taking it into the world and testing it.

Going Forward: Journal Entries

Gregory Landua

I will continue to dedicate time to reflection on the essence of the economic shaper role, and I will invite my team to do the same. We clearly need to continue to explore and uncover the basic infrastructural building blocks for a regenerative economy: democratic engagement, participation in design and decision making, and agency in service to the health of the systems we depend on. Growing these depends on the practice of this essence-based role. It's like exercising a basic muscle of humanness.

Amanda Pinelli

I find myself thinking on my own in quiet time about how to apply the economic shaper essence. In the heat of the moment I'm rarely able to hold it present, but at other times I apply it without even realizing it, which reveals itself later when I reflect on my experience. I believe that the vision of systems of real wealth, evolution, and the infrastructures to support evolution will always be a part of my work.

It's been particularly useful to stay aware of inner obstacles, without getting so caught up in the psychological why or how. It also helps me support my interlocutors when they get caught up in these obstacles. It's evident how important it is to meet people where they are, speaking a language they can understand and supporting them in building their infrastructure of knowledge for regeneration.

Ricardo Peón

An important gain for me has been to connect through the research project with like-minded people working on the same issues. The fact that there were other people trying to work in the same field as me and facing similar difficulties, such as communicating a regenerative vision to others, was encouraging. Realizing that I was working on something relatively unexplored changed from an obstacle to a challenging opportunity. I can see the potential for a dialogue among a group of economic shapers to help evolve the ideas we are all trying to advance. Accessing this community would be of great value to me, and I hope it would be for all of us!

Additional Insight: Journal Entry

Research participant Kevin Jones, who lives on a farm near Asheville, North Carolina, is a cofounder of GatherLAB and SOCAP, both of which focus on social impact through innovations in investment. One of his recent projects included Somali immigrants in and around Minneapolis, where he was attempting to structure a program that would aid community members to access the capital they needed to purchase homes. He very quickly learned that American concepts of ownership, debt, and investment were alien to Somali culture. Using the economic shaper essence triad to inform his thinking, he set out to coinvent with these immigrants a new and more appropriate financial model. He explained in his journal that

> Somalis keep their community giving and their investing in different pockets. Their culture frowns on the concept of interest, which they see as making money on money and thereby creating a systemic preference for the rich. This causes them to feel uncomfortable working within the American banking system. Also, when they invest they expect a modest return and are willing to think in terms of 15-year paybacks. So we created a fund in which 200 people contributed $2,500 a piece in order to enable two of their neighbors to purchase their first homes. It's essentially a crowd-funding approach by which the community leverages its purchasing power to address its own needs. This makes perfect sense from the Somali cultural outlook, for after all, they've been investing in their collective future forever because nobody else was going to do it for them.
>
> This process taught me that my ideas were based in my own culture and didn't necessarily fit the way Somali Americans and other immigrant communities see the world. Although my ideas might work brilliantly somewhere else, they didn't in the Somali community, which has its own character, its own culture, and its own ways of working. I had to be quiet and hear what wasn't making sense to them. My listening enabled us to bring our goodwill together in order to create something they want to continue to be part of.
>
> In the process, we also learned that some of our "social investment" allies couldn't understand this very different way of thinking— the idea that community members would be willing to invest in a collective future. As part of longer-standing American financial traditions, these allies are currently wedded to a private-property, invest-for-myself-not-the-community mind-set. Clearly, there's plenty of potential for regeneration when new ideas are contributed by people who see things differently.

CHAPTER TEN

The Regenerative Educator Role

M OST PEOPLE associate the word *educator* with professional teachers working in classrooms. Indeed, some educators are teachers, but the term is much broader than this in its meaning, and many of us play the role of educator in various aspects of our lives.

The root word is the Latin *educare*, which means "to draw out or draw through." To educate someone is to draw out of them their inner potential for intelligence and wisdom. True educators don't teach people *what* to think. Rather, they teach them *how* to think. Education is a process of disruption and liberation that enables students to develop the critical thinking necessary for forming thoughts and judgments independently. It is our primary resource for maturation and the development of agency.

A regenerative educator renounces the role of expert or holder of knowledge. This is because the transfer of knowledge may increase the amount of stuff in students' memories, but it doesn't create fundamental changes in the way they process what's in their minds. To do this requires the development of understanding through consciously engaged experience. An educator must challenge students to let go of their certainty so that they can make real discoveries. Students must learn to generate meaning from experience; this is why effective educators make a point of providing learners with opportunities for usefully challenging experiences.

Related to this idea, a regenerative educator invites learners to engage in discernment in order to make their own determination about the validity of ideas. Students are expected to test the ideas that they encounter or generate, neither accepting nor rejecting them until they've verified them through their own investigation. This is a critical foundation to independent thought, the opposite of depending on an outside authority to deliver the *right* ideas or ways of thinking.

Regenerative educators know to their cores that they are undertaking their own ongoing processes of development. The relationship between educator and learner is one of mutual engagement, designed to generate new knowledge for both. Learning to draw out and develop the intelligence of others is a lifelong task, one that true educators find both stimulating and nourishing. This always involves encountering the mystery that is the soul of another person, and such encounters invariably change us, no matter how often they occur.

An interesting phenomenon that showed up in the regenerative life project was the many participants playing other roles who discovered that they needed to incorporate the role of educator in order to be effective at the regenerative level. For example, regenerative parents inevitably also serve as educators for their own children and often for many others. Regenerative entrepreneurs need to build capability and capacity in their teams, distribution channels, and even markets if they are to successfully disrupt an industry. This capacity-building dimension is inherent to regenerative work, and so it seems natural that the educator role supports all of the other roles.

The Essence of the Regenerative Educator

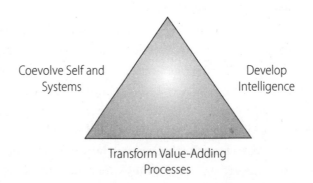

Coevolve Self and
Systems

Develop
Intelligence

Transform Value-Adding
Processes

In the case of the regenerative educator, the core process is to *develop intelligence*, the core purpose is to *transform value-adding processes*, and the core value is to *coevolve self and systems*. Intelligence, as it is conventionally understood, refers to the amount of knowledge a person has acquired and can readily access—this is the kind of intelligence for which students are generally tested. In a regenerative context, intelligence refers to the ability to gain a dynamic, systemic understanding of a situation, and then apply and extend this understanding to making skillful interventions that will upgrade the situation's outcomes. *Development* is the ongoing process of discovering and manifesting the inherent potential of something or someone. *Developing intelligence* integrates gaining knowledge and experience with the ability to manage one's motivation and state of being, so that what has been experienced can provide the basis for understanding and wise action. This is, of course, the work of a lifetime, because this kind of intelligence is not quantitative and fixed but continuously growing and deepening.

Value-adding processes are how we channel the innate drive to make our lives meaningful into contributions toward improving the world in some way. I believe that this is a nearly universal compulsion in human beings and human institutions. For example, businesses exist to provide products and services for people, and most parents seek ways to make life better for their children. However, the forms that this drive to create value can take often become severely distorted through lack of systemic intelligence. When we *transform value-adding processes*, we change both their forms and their effects, so that the living systems we engage with become more coherent and true to themselves. This, I believe, is the appropriate—and, really, the inevitable use of—intelligence that has been developed through regenerative education.

When we develop intelligence toward transforming value-adding processes, we are changed by our efforts to improve some system. That is, we *coevolve self and systems* in a profoundly interdependent way. This directly contradicts the popular notion that we need to work on self-actualization or healing before we set out to change the world. In a regenerative educational process, the effort to make systems better becomes the context and energy source for self-actualizing. This is true for both participants and educators—everyone learns to disrupt and evolve the systems they are part of as the means to develop themselves.

Experiencing the Regenerative Educator Role

Sharon Molloy works in a small rural school system in southern New Mexico, teaching eight- to eleven-year-old children with learning disabilities and behavioral challenges. She is both passionate and skillful in this role, but prior to her participation in the project, she had recently faced an exceptionally difficult year, which she described in her journal:

> Behavioral issues were increasing, not decreasing. Students were openly contemptuous of me and other teachers, and they were passively defiant. It was hard to get through any kind of direct instruction without disruption. For the first time in my teaching life, I was sending kids to the office over behavior issues. I no longer looked forward to the school day; my joy in teaching had evaporated. As things got worse, my perspective narrowed. I kept returning to the idea of constancy—consistent rules and consistent consequences. I thought that if I could just get better at being consistent at application of the rules and consequences (never my strong suit), the problem would be solved.
>
> When I saw the Levels of Paradigm Framework, I realized that the dark tunnel I was experiencing was actually a manifestation of a transactional, value-return mind-set. In the face of this very challenging environment, my view of what I was doing as an educator had collapsed to just getting through the lessons for a given day. Recognizing this helped open up a larger view, and I felt my inspiration return.
>
> I was particularly struck by the articulation of the core process of education as *develop intelligence*. It immediately became apparent to me that the so-called behavioral problems I was focused on were actually opportunities for developing the children's (and my) intelligence with regard to personal self-management and self-mastery.
>
> The next day, I noted in my journal that although nothing overt had changed, the mood in the classroom was different. It was as though the students sensed a change in me and were responding in kind. At one point, Kendra was trying to address me, and kept calling me by other "M" names: "Mom, no (giggle), Mollie, no (giggle), Ms. Molloy..." We all laughed, and Justin—one of my most challenging students—turned to me, looked deep into my eyes, and said "Are you our mom?" Later,

upon reflecting, I realized that only one out of all my students has an intact relationship with his mother.

Later the same day, Sharon was able to apply this insight, along with her understanding of the core purpose of the educator role—*transform value-adding processes*—to an interaction with a student named Mollie. Like all of the children in Sharon's classroom, Mollie is at an age where she is trying to discover her value, the contributions that she will one day make as she learns to navigate her world and future. Sharon again chose to make the essence framework her compass.

> The whole school was rehearsing the Christmas program. Mollie rolled her eyes, refusing to listen to her drama coach. I motioned for her to come talk with me, and I took her aside. Before, I would have given "the warning." Instead, I saw the essence triad in my mind and told her that I had noticed that she has a powerful presence onstage, that she is not afraid to speak loudly and clearly, and that other people tend to follow her lead. I said that I believed she could develop these abilities further and mentioned that I was concerned that if she formed a habit of ignoring or being contemptuous of coaching from adults in charge of productions, it might limit her opportunities.
>
> When we began the conversation, her arms were crossed and she had a scowl on her face. Everything about her body language said, "Keep out!" But as I spoke, her face opened and changed, like a flower unfurling. She nodded her head, said "I understand," went back onstage, and was fully engaged through the rest of the rehearsal.

A few days later, Sharon engaged her students in a deep and reflective conversation about their relationships with one another, their teachers, and their parents. The discouraging patterns that she had encountered earlier in the year were affecting everyone, and she wanted to help the children build a baseline for how they could do a better job of managing themselves. She described this to me as a memorable event, a mutual opening that they could collectively refer back to when things got tough in the classroom.

For Sharon, this was a chance to experience the core value of the educator role, *coevolve self and systems*. On the one hand, she was helping the kids become more accountable for themselves as a way of working successfully within their school and family systems. But equally important, she was gaining new insight about how to evolve the systems she is part of. She noted in her journal,

> Part of this "opening up" has included becoming aware of sources of nurturance, inspiration, and connection that had been invisible to me. For example, parents and community members began to show up with skills to offer—or perhaps I began to see and connect with them in a different way. Engaging in my work from the educator role's core value, to coevolve self and systems, expands the scope of my work from classroom to school, community, and larger world.

Finding the Right Level

Shelly Pottorf is an assistant professor in the School of Architecture at Prairie View A&M University in Texas, which has traditionally served African American students. In recent years, she has been teaching a regenerative design course that includes a group project on behalf of a low-income neighborhood in her city. This has revealed a number of inherent tensions between her training as an architect and the need to adopt a fundamentally different approach, for the benefit of her students as well as her community. As she puts it,

> I have an analytical mind that easily discerns problems and lays out the most efficient method for arriving at the "right" solution. The practice of architecture has been codified into a "set-the-problem, solve-the-problem" framework, which is a perfect example of the arrest disorder paradigm. I know that this is at odds with the creative process, but I happen to be kind of good at it. So it is difficult for me to avoid reverting to it when the pressure is on.
>
> In addition, architectural education exhibits a strong bias toward outcomes over process. In other words, at the end of the day what really matters is the product rather than any learning and development that

might occur along the way. Five years ago, when I first started teaching, this was my primary operating framework. Success was gauged in terms of knowledge transfer as evidenced by the final product. The actual development of intelligence within the student was hardly considered.

My desire to work from the Regenerate Life Paradigm has forced me to take a good hard look at why I teach. The potential of a historically black university is to create the conditions in which students and faculty can self-actualize without having to overcome barriers that are typically present in society at large. If in addition I can link my students' self-actualization to system actualization, then they will be well equipped to address the persistent diversity issues that continue to plague the architectural profession. Even more important, they will be able to proactively address the profession's struggle to serve minority populations and communities.

It is clear to me that I need to disrupt the status quo. It's also clear how often I fail and how miserably! My taskmaster takes over, especially when I know that a class has an important deliverable that has been promised to the community. I become afraid that the students might fail to deliver the project, even though I know that not allowing for failure is a backhanded way of cutting us off from our essence and potential. I can go unconscious and start to take over some of the students' responsibilities. In these ways, I buy into the old paradigm that the project is what's important, rather than the development of people. Through my participation in the regenerative life research project, I knew that managing *me* was going to be my biggest challenge.

When the end of the semester came around, I was prepared to allow things to unfold. The final deliverable was a 10-minute video telling the story of the neighborhood we work with. I knew that my students were way behind, and I went into the final presentation with low expectations, reframing this for myself as a milestone within an ongoing work in progress. By the time class started, the video still wasn't done. So while we waited for the person working on the video to finish, we reflected on the class in general and how to continue regenerative work in the world.

Then a heated conversation between two students broke out in the back of the classroom. Soon it pulled in everyone's attention. Basically, they had resorted to finger-pointing about why the presentation wasn't done and why the quality wasn't where it could have been. Everyone in the class started to chime in. I had to make a choice.

What I chose was to not interfere. I decided in that moment that this was the deep personal work that was really being asked of them. My job was to let it play out. I needed to take on a resource role, dedicated to developing my students' systemic intelligence in this moment. I listened in a nonjudgmental, non-reactionary way. I didn't allow myself to get sucked in but instead created a reflective space for everyone to explore a triggered state of being.

Eventually, one of the conflict's instigators asked me to take his side. I didn't. I instead pointed to the lessons on self-reflection, internal locus of control, and external considering. I took right-and-wrong off the table and encouraged everyone to use this conflict as an opportunity to work on these new skills of self-management. I encouraged them to reflect on how their own personal engagement throughout the process right up to that moment either did or did not serve our intentions for the team and the project. These conversations continued after class and over the next couple of days.

Incidentally, the project ended up being a pretty decent first draft. Even better, a group of students signed up to continue working on it after the end of the semester.

Applying the Seven First Principles

Brandon Costelloe-Kuehn teaches design students at Rensselaer Polytechnic Institute in Troy, New York, where he has experimented over the years with how to craft contexts for developmental experiences. Nevertheless, his participation in the research for this book revealed a relatively unexplored opportunity to make student evaluation a far more developmental and self-accountable process. In Brandon's words:

Before the research project, I often asked students to offer feedback on each other's work. But I had never placed self-evaluation at the center of the process in a way that could take into account the individual, specific, and unique background, positioning, and potential of each student. I always struggled to know each individual student as best I could, a daunting task with as many as 100 new students each semester. But I had never taken full advantage of how well they know themselves; nor had I offered experiences that could help deepen this self-knowledge. I wanted students to take their education personally, including grading themselves.

Brandon knew that he was going to have to address a tricky problem if he took this approach. He wanted students who were seriously invested in their education, for whom self-evaluation could enhance learning. But he knew that there was a real chance that the approach he was taking could attract students who wanted to game the system.

I didn't want students to take my classes simply because they heard it was an easy A. By getting away from a focus on grading (in a standard way, by the professor), I could ironically end up with a bunch of students who were taking the class *because* of a focus on grading. On top of that, grade-motivated students could crowd out students who have a legitimate interest in the classes. As a primary goal, getting an A seems like a perfect example of what it means to operate from the value return paradigm. It certainly isn't consistent with the regenerative approach I was trying to introduce.

After wrestling with this question for a while, Brandon decided to commit himself fully to student self-evaluation.

I asked students to hold themselves accountable and evaluate their work in relation to their own understanding of their evolving and specific potential. As a way of keeping them honest, I asked them to take self-evaluation very seriously and informed them that anything less than forthcoming, accurate, and thorough assessments could have a major negative impact on their overall grade.

The outcomes of this self-evaluation process were incredible. Students seemed to really build their capacity to take responsibility, not in a self-flagellating, finger-wagging kind of way, but in the sense of an ability to respond based on their specific situations. In addition, students made great strides in developing the intelligence required for understanding themselves in terms of their nestedness in larger systems (including the system of higher education). Many students naturally identified multiple, interlocked inner obstacles, even though I hadn't offered them this precise language (something I will certainly do next semester). Students were also incredibly honest and accurate in their evaluations. I was quite surprised that the only modifications I had to make were to increase a few of the students' grades because often students from less privileged backgrounds had been overly harsh toward themselves.

It is not difficult to recognize the seven first principles of regeneration in Brandon's story. First of all, he thinks of his students as *whole* human beings, with their own *essence* and *potential*. By allowing students to have their own unique starting points and their own learning processes, he avoided the fragmentation and dehumanization associated with typical grading processes, which locate students in relation to one another on a curve. He also built new energy and potential into the process by giving students full responsibility, while setting a boundary to prevent anyone gaming the system.

This provided just enough containment to create a *field* within which students could give themselves fully to *developing* (and monitoring) themselves. As a result, the students (and the school itself) became quite conscious that they were participating in a radical challenge to the teaching profession's usual practice. This helped students maintain a high degree of awareness of the *nested* systems (self, classroom, institute, higher education) that they were influencing and being influenced by.

Finally, the *nodal* opportunity that Brandon intuitively recognized was to bring together three processes—ideation, creation, and evaluation—that have been split apart to the detriment of nearly every aspect of modern life. The fragmentation and devaluation of human beings arising from this split has undermined the potential of all of our institutions, from families and schools to businesses and governments. Brandon's insight was both simple and profound. For students to become whole and integrated human beings, they needed to take responsibility for—and indeed to insist upon responsibility for—all three.

Managing Inner Obstacles

Maya—who prefers not to use her last name here—is an educator and head of innovation at a school in north London. She has struggled to reconcile the conflict between her own sense of what it means to be an effective educator and the demands of her department to produce tangible, measurable outcomes. At the time she joined the regenerative life research project, this conflict had become acute, to the point that she actually feared she might lose her job. As she put it in her journal,

> We were working on a social innovation project. My plan was to use design thinking as a basis for community engagement and project development, as well as for an inner journey in which students would identify their learnings and the evolution of their being. I was keen to explore using this approach, as it resonates with my understanding of what education should be. I deeply believe that self-discovery and understanding, which come through conscious, experiential learning, result in longer-lasting skills and transformations.
>
> However, I was immediately faced with pushback from both students and staff. "Your methods will not produce tangible results—having students account for their own learning is too unreliable. And there is no preexisting project underway." In a meeting with the department head, I was asked to demonstrate proof that learning would happen.
>
> I absorbed their doubts and fears, mixing them with my own inner obstacles (which were already strong, given that I was in a new role, feeling like I was in hostile territory, and needing to show success quickly to get buy-in). As a result, I shut down my own thinking, my own innate knowledge and beliefs, and reverted to trying to show some kind of tangible deliverable. I began to design the program to suit department expectations.

As Maya became more conscious of the inner obstacles that were at work in her, she began to find ways to manage them so that she could get back on course and serve the education of her students rather than the fears of her institution:

First, I identified the effect of *attachment* on me. I could see that I had unconsciously adopted the beliefs that the environment and status quo of university education is fixed and that I have to adapt to succeed within it. With this realization, I reminded myself that I was brought in to create something new, with a new language and framework, and that this is important and necessary to the long-term health of the university. I began to reframe my project in line with the changes that I think we need to see in education.

I also struggle with *fabrication*. I suspect that many of the perceived issues of resistance within the school are actually being imagined by me. I particularly have to be on guard against *fear*, especially the fear of getting fired for not toeing the line. I realize now that the best way to get fired from my position is to abandon my own experience and sense of what is right and effective for students. Going forward, my real work is to articulate the value of my approach within the overall principles and goals of the university, and this is a work in progress.

Generating a New Pattern

Rachel Greenberger is the cofounder of Food Sol, a program housed within the Lewis Institute at Babson College, a Boston-area business school specializing in entrepreneurship. The institute focuses on social innovation, helping businesses in the United States grow their effectiveness as change makers. After graduating from Babson, Rachel teamed up with Cheryl Kiser, executive director of the institute, because they wanted to create a program focused on innovation with regard to every aspect of the American food system.

In addition to creating platforms and events designed to stimulate innovation within the food industry, Food Sol works with graduate students interested in making this their area of focus. Thus, Rachel finds herself in the role of educator in her work with food-related businesses and entrepreneurs, as well as within Babson's academic programs. But on reflection, she realized that she was playing the role at a pretty low level.

I often feel pressed to be an expert, to earn my keep by proving that my presence has value. I am well aware of the professorial game, which is based on capital "K" Knowing. When students come to you with questions, they believe your answers. This is the root story of academia. Most people live by it, whether or not their particular answers fit a particular student.

When it comes to food, I am recognized as someone who knows a lot of people and a lot of things and who studies the industry daily. Naturally, students come to me looking for direction, advice, and contacts. If they come in quick succession, I tend to feel bombarded. Under pressure, I default to just pushing out answers. "Here's a carrot. Now go away."

This has never felt particularly great, but I've *always* thought it was my job to dole out answers, based on my expertise, as efficiently as possible. I've believed that I was being helpful. When I've been energetically tapped out, I've also seen it as a way to move people along, like an assembly line, so that I can get back to whatever big, quiet-time project I'm working on. Whenever a student is excited or grateful for the loot I hand over, I consider it a good outcome, pat myself on the back, and move on to the next student.

For Rachel, participation in the research for this book was revelatory.

One of Carol's assertions caused me to completely rethink the way I was working with students. She said, "Everything alive has the ability to regenerate what it is uniquely." She went on to unpack one of the implications of this idea, which is that from a regenerative point of view there are no commodities.

This led me to reexamine my image of an "assembly line" of graduate students waiting at my door to have new parts and pieces installed. This queue of students is *not* an assembly line, but a powerful array of precious, one-of-a-kind beings, every one of whom holds a unique power and potential to influence food and industry.

Getting more caring people into the business of transforming food is the reason I got into my work in the first place. So I've been trying a different mind-set, a different lens, even though it feels a little risky because I am not following the root story of academia. The results have been noteworthy and encouraging. For example, in preparation for a visit from a second-year MBA student whom I know well, I began by grounding my energy. I knew that I needed to center myself if I was to practice the level of silence I intended. I wanted to let the student lead the conversation. I also wanted the courage to leave spacious pauses in our exchange so that she could continue her line of thinking—a line that is typically cut off too soon in the high-speed back-and-forth that is typical of business culture.

Being clear, empty—or at least emptier than usual—and present, I refrained from interrupting and from the nervous habit of rushing to fill pauses. This created a profound result. The student both asked the questions and answered them. She went further in revealing and voicing her insights than ever before. I had left her the space for it! She was deeply listened to, which is its own form of teaching.

This student sensed the difference in the nature of our meeting and commented on it. She talked about feeling clearer and retuned. At the end of the conversation, I gave her resources for the new plans she had formed, rather than for the ones she'd walked in with. What surprised me most about this new approach was how energy conserving it was. I was trying something new—which can easily be tiring—and getting potent results. I left the encounter refreshed!

Going Forward: Journal Entries

Shelly Pottorf

I've distilled what I learned into three principles to guide me going forward.

- Provide the learning environment and guidance that helps each student discover their essence and unique gifts.
- Incorporate self-reflective processes as the framework through which all other work is pursued.
- Design projects to facilitate the formation and development of guilds that will pursue the project. Make the development of people primary and the project secondary.

Brandon Costelloe-Kuehn

I plan to push my experiment further by utilizing self-evaluation processes throughout the entire semester and giving students a greater degree of freedom to develop their own criteria for evaluation.

What surprised me, blew me away even, was how readily that self-actualizing and system-actualizing work came together in this process. I'm inspired by the great task of bringing my values into greater alignment with my everyday choices. I'm excited about helping students shift from seeing values as a form of moralistic drudgery to an exploration of how individual purpose and will can resonate with biospheric health and wellness.

Maya

I will keep these insights in mind as I reevaluate next term's design. I want to ensure that there is sufficient space and time for learning by doing, developing key questions to unlock the intelligence in students, and supporting the practice of reflection. I aim to create high-quality project results, while also ensuring that the full selves of students can be expressed. In addition, I will continue to clarify and articulate my values and paradigms so that they will advance rather than hinder the program.

Rachel Greenberger

I want to establish a new pattern in my relationship with students. I've committed to arrive at meetings armed with nothing but a few great questions, questions that are deliberately spacious, are inherently philosophical, and require a bit of wrestling in order to understand. I'm also committed to meditating before meetings, practicing silence, and leaning back to create more space, physical and energetic, for the other person.

After all, if everyone is a unique being, then any predetermined, formulaic process is going to get really clunky, really quick. Space feels *essential* to generating clarity in the one seeking to be drawn out.

Additional Insight: Journal Entry

Geoff Stack, another program participant, is GIVE fellowship leader with Business Volunteers of Maryland in Baltimore. The fellowship is a 10-month capability-building program, with the aim to prepare rising leaders who are "motivated and passionate about making a difference in their community and career." While Geoff was participating in the regenerative life project, he was also designing the structure and content of workshops for the 2019 fellowship cohort, the majority of whom were women working in the corporate sector. He explains in his journal:

> I am an educator, even though I'm not working with what people usually think of as students. GIVE fellows are professionals, 25 to 40 years old, ready to take their community engagement to the next level. They are focused on building their personal and professional networks, and have only about 5 to 10 hours a month to give to the fellowship.
>
> This was the first year that I undertook the lead role in designing workshops for the program. One of the main lessons I'll take away from the research project is that true educating requires the engagement of everyone—not just participants but my teaching collaborators as well. I see an opportunity to evolve the program as a whole in order to fully embrace the working of the Regenerate Life Paradigm throughout the fellowship year. By educating collaborators and fellows about a living systems perspective, we all become more conscious of when we're moving between different levels of paradigm. This gives everyone a way to watch paradigms at work.

CHAPTER ELEVEN

The Regenerative Media Content Creator Role

I N OUR MEDIA-SATURATED information age, the role of the media content creator enjoys an astonishing level of potential to move or influence every aspect of society. This has led to unprecedented global connectedness and awareness of large-scale systemic phenomena, such as climate change. It has also led to widespread manipulations, "alternative" facts, repetitive cinematic blockbusters, and a media echo chamber that elevates a few events to national or international importance, while drowning out almost everything else.

These observations aren't new. They are themselves bromides, repeated over and over in the broadcast media (which, like most of us, loves to talk about itself). They suggest that although media creators have become ultrasophisticated, they've lost contact with the underlying purposes that should guide their role. Without a coherent sense of its social purpose, the industry (along with ordinary social media users) just keeps pumping out more and more content on a faster and faster cycle with less and less beneficial result. This is the definition of *pollutant*, a resource entering a system at a faster rate than it can be absorbed and metabolized.

I define *media* as mass communication, the sources most people use regularly to keep themselves informed: publishing, broadcasting, and the

Internet. I believe that mass communication has three basic tasks. The first and most fundamental is to transmit information in order to facilitate the generation of knowledge. The second task is to provide us with experience—this is the role of artful storytelling and powerful imagery. The third is to activate agency through rhetorical means, such as persuasion and exhortation. Advanced media practitioners become highly skilled at combining these three practices. For example, the power of well-crafted propaganda or advertising is that it conveys carefully selected information within an emotionally compelling experience designed to trigger action (or inaction) on the part of its audience.

When we look at the media content creator role through the lens of regeneration, these three tasks shift their focus from manipulation to self-determination. Regenerative media content creators work to lift their audiences from gathering knowledge to generating understanding by helping them discern patterns and principles underlying what they observe in the world. These content creators offer powerful experiences— for example, of what it's like to be people very different from ourselves by hearing their stories and imaging ourselves into their shoes—in order to cultivate compassion and wisdom. Media content generators encourage agency, but of a kind that is discerning and self-generated rather than reflexive and unquestioning.

The Essence of the Regenerative Media Content Creator

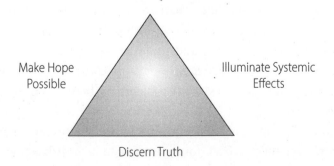

Make Hope Possible

Illuminate Systemic Effects

Discern Truth

For the role of regenerative media content creator, the core process is to *illuminate systemic effects*. Media creators at this level are almost always fascinated by the question "How did we get here?" They know that many threads have come together to give rise to whatever crazy phenomena they may be observing and that their first task is to assemble a systemic picture of underlying patterns at work. This brings artistry to the fore and inspires the creation of stories and images with the power to illuminate what is otherwise invisible—the patterns of interaction that are evolving, arresting, or devolving systems.

The role's core purpose is to *discern truth*. What we perceive depends on where we're standing, our point of view. Life tends to teach us that even a simple shift in perspective can radically alter what we thought was true, a popular theme in novels and films. One implication of this is that looking at what we observe from multiple perspectives allows us to assemble an increasingly whole understanding of what is true. Another is that shifting levels, moving from a close-in perspective to one that is regional or national or even planetary, can also help us deepen and enrich our understanding. Truth is the subjective pursuit of ever-expanding and encompassing ways of seeing and comprehending, rather than a collective drilling down to organized lists of objective facts. This is why the work is to *discern* the truth, to test it, explore it, and engage it in a rigorous, disciplined, but unattached way. The regenerative media content creator understands that this is the work of us all and offers ideas, images, insights, and questions as means to help us work on our own discernment.

The role's core value is to *make hope possible*. Hope comes from the ability to see another path or possibility when the path we are on becomes closed. Hope dies when we can see no way out or forward. This is because agency is a core aspect of what it means to be human. We all want to have an effect on our worlds and to change what we see needs changing. When these avenues of action and contribution are closed to us, we deflate, and our energies curdle into passivity, resentment, and self-defeat.

This is one reason why the current media environment can be poisonous, setting the stage for apathy, demagoguery, and autocratic leadership that is more than willing to take control of an audience's or constituency's agency. A regenerative media content creator stimulates active imagination and will, revealing the many options that are actually available to us if we continually question expertise and authority, and if we allow our agency to be guided by our own discernment.

Experiencing the Regenerative Media Content Creator Role

Tonya Mosley is an award-winning journalist based in Los Angeles whose aim is to find and expose truths for the greater good of society. She is cohost of National Public Radio's *Here and Now* and the creator of *Truth Be Told*, an advice show made by and for people of color. She shared the following reflections about the significance of the content creator's essence triad for her own work as a journalist.

> I think it's easier to stay focused on the idea of *discerning truth* in the context of a podcast like *Truth Be Told*, where I have the freedom to pursue points of view in a deeper way because I'm not bounded by the preoccupations of mainstream media. As a journalist, I always try to shed light on different worlds, to give people a context from which to view a world beyond my own. I am a product of Western society, and so I have to open myself. I have to move beyond the simplistic, two-sides-of-a-story idea and invite my audience to look a bit deeper. This is a bigger challenge with a program like *Here and Now* because we have to work fast to meet regular deadlines.
>
> I'm challenged in the same way when it comes to *making hope possible*. This is my aspiration, something I am constantly pursuing. But fostering hope requires being able to slow down your thinking so that you can be intentional, keeping it at the center of your work. The human brain is always looking for shortcuts that make work faster and more efficient. I might start out wanting to act from a place of heart but end up pushing just to get the information out there, which is a persistent problem in journalism. Because it fails to provide context, today's media is almost always only two-dimensional.

When I was working at Al Jazeera America, I did a series about a young transgender student in middle school who, along with their parents, was fighting for gender-neutral bathrooms in schools. I spoke with them about their transition and the need to have safe spaces and be included at school, where they spent the majority of their time. I can see now how much my mind-set has evolved over time and how much deeper my understanding has gotten.

This young student helped me learn how to convey their truth, as well as the truth of society, as it has evolved over the last few years. I realize how much I've grown in my ability, not just to provide facts but also to help develop the understanding of context and give listeners a sense of the living complexity in one person's story.

Finding the Right Level

Emma Morris lives on Waiheke Island, New Zealand, where she is part of the founding team for Tuia Learning Environment, which offers learning experiences that equip people and communities to adapt to fast-changing conditions. When she joined the regenerative life research project, she was coauthoring an article on the organization, which led her to some important insights about how her team was using language.

I had teamed up with a colleague to respond to a request for an article from a polytechnic institute in our region. In our first draft the Arrest Disorder and Do Good paradigms were strongly represented. We were focused on current problems, advocating "changing mind-sets" because people were thinking in the "wrong way." We proposed a "right way" that should be imposed.

After my introduction to the four paradigms, I started to see many patterns in our language—in the article and in the ways we talk about the organization generally—that reflected the lower levels. I wanted to shift the language so that it communicated the regenerative intention that's implicit in our vision. What surprised me was that when I attempted to explain this to the rest of the team, I kept falling back into arresting disorder and doing good. Clearly it's a deep part of my conditioning, and I observed the same pattern in the language used by others. I thought that we were all solid on our vision, but I couldn't help but notice the discrepancies between it and how we were describing it.

As a result, I believe I am starting to more authentically and deeply understand what our vision statements mean and how the learning environment will need to operate in order to live up to them. By experiencing the distinction between the Do Good Paradigm and the Regenerate Life Paradigm, I've also gotten more clarity on how the essence and vision of the organization can resonate within the learning experiences we offer.

Applying the Seven First Principles

Shannon Murphy lives in Santa Fe, New Mexico, where she is the communications director for Regenesis Group, a development consultancy, and the Regenesis Institute for Regenerative Practice, an educational nonprofit. She has been working on the design and launch of an online platform for students and practitioners associated with the institute.

At first I assumed that I was creating a conventional website, onto which we could invite regenerative practitioners to describe the work they were doing in the world. This would build a growing archive of interesting projects and help the community get its voice heard, while teaching the public about regenerative development. I saw that there were a ton of people interested in the subject, but doing a full training was too much for them, so I wanted to offer bite-sized pieces that would create more literacy about regenerative ideas. But when I framed it this way, the concept never got traction. It just didn't seem important enough to devote the requisite time and resources.

Seeing the content creator's essence triad reminded me that I needed to lift my thinking about this project up to the regenerate life level. My first breakthrough came when I stopped seeing myself as a journalist collecting good stories. Instead of creating videos and articles and podcasts, my team would serve as resources to all of these practitioners, helping them create their own media content in their own voices and from their own perspectives. Our task shifted to working *developmentally* with our content creators, while simultaneously articulating the meta-framing that would allow their diversity to remain coherent.

My second breakthrough came when I began to see that our work is *nested* within a larger *field* of systems change, a global movement of diverse organizations, theorists, and activists. This is the greater *whole* that we are part of, and we need to become more skillful at engaging with it. Like us, these thinkers and practitioners are motivated by an urgent sense that humans need to change quickly and radically in terms of how they coexist with one another and their planet. I believe that regenerative development has much to offer this movement, if we can find *nodal* ways to contribute.

Of course, this requires staying mindful of both the *essence* of the movement and the *essence* of regenerative development, so that what we contribute remains authentic and distinctive. We especially need to be evolving our own understanding of regenerative development and its *potential* in the world. This is why I speak of meta-framing. As a living-systems approach to change, regeneration is still an emerging theory and discipline, with a great need for experimentation, refinement, and discovery of new applications. Without overarching frameworks to guide this work, it could easily lose its rigor and intelligence and become indistinguishable from a host of other sustainability or systems-change methods.

So I'm now thinking of the platform as a way to resource the development of the people we serve. Our practitioners come from many different fields, working on everything from the built environment to community development to impact investment to education. Each of them has great potential, and they keep showing up because they see potential in the world, which they want to actualize. What their stories reveal is that the core of the change will come from elevations in the way they see things. What they've manifested as specific projects is far less important than the higher order of potential that they are now able to perceive and pursue.

Here's an example. We've been working for more than a decade with a network of practitioners centered in Mexico City. They include architects, planners, teachers, biologists, business leaders, and financial experts. All are passionately committed to the positive transformation of their city and their nation, but until recently the results of this work were hard to see. They were mostly engaged in trying to figure out how to apply a regenerative approach to their respective endeavors and how to build or borrow platforms from which it would be possible to create influence.

Now these efforts are beginning to surface. One group is beginning to shift the philosophy and policy of the city with regard to how it manages its water supply. Another is challenging the nation's top industrial council to rethink the paradigms it's operating from. Another has enlisted a skilled group of stakeholders to commit to regenerating the watershed of Valle de Bravo. These are just a few of the initiatives that are bubbling up, as a band of people who are teaching themselves how to look at things differently is starting to resource real change.

Managing Inner Obstacles

Dan Palmer is an ecological designer and educator living in Central Victoria, Australia, where he hosts a website, podcast, and video series called *Making Permaculture Stronger*. He was intrigued by the idea of applying the regenerative life frameworks to the ways he conceived and carried out interviews for his podcast. The experiment has profoundly shifted his approach to interviews in the future, but along the way Dan had the opportunity to recognize and struggle with some of his inner obstacles.

For my first try, I decided that the subject of the podcast was one whole that I was working with and the audience was the other. I tried to image the subject and the audience, thinking about ways to steer the conversation so that it could be accessible and open up levels of meaning. The interview went okay, but the only real change was that I paid more attention than usual to making it usable for listeners.

A few days later the penny dropped. I realized that there was nothing specific and concrete about the idea of listeners, in the sense that I couldn't know and be in touch with them as I recorded a conversation. I therefore couldn't help but project my own *fabrications*. Basically I was making my audience up and talking to a projected version of myself. It dawned on me (in a way that makes me feel kind of stupid now) that the concrete, specific whole I was working with was my guest! I realized that I could focus on *a guest's* uniqueness or essence and invite it into the space of our conversation.

As I reflected on the content creator's core purpose, discerning truth, I also realized that I have tended to meet people where they are, which determines where we hang out and what we explore. Yet I know I have the capacity to tease out different layers of understanding and invite others into exploring them.

As a result of these two realizations, recording the next podcast was a profoundly different experience. I began by generating the beginnings of a framework to explore together with my interviewee. Then, during our recorded conversation, I invited her to explore and coevolve it with me. She accepted, and so there we were, explicitly exploring the patterns in her work and the different layers of truth they pointed to.

It was a beautiful and illuminating experience for me. What I loved was that there was no judgment in it, no sense that any of the layers either of us suggested was either good or bad. What I also loved was that it genuinely helped frame so much of what this person stands for and how she works, as well as new spheres of possibility to be explored. It went so far beyond learning only about her specific practices and projects.

Early in the recording, when I first introduced the framework, my guest made a comment that I didn't like. I reflected afterward that this involved both *identification* and subjectivism (not to mention working from the Do Good Paradigm). I had identified with my framework and its importance and felt like *I* was being made to look bad when critical comments were made about something that *I* had suggested. I caught myself in the moment and returned my attention to being present to my guest's essence, rather than worrying about how I was coming across. Later, I realized that a framework doesn't need to be understood and grabbed instantly. It's better to think of it as a conversation starter and a source for perspective-widening questions. It frames our thinking together.

Generating a New Pattern

David McConville is cofounder of Spherical, an integrative research and design strategy studio based in Oakland, California, which focuses on developing tools and techniques for regenerating the health and integrity of Earth's living systems. At the time of the regenerative life research project, he was working on a program to help artists create experiential spaces for the public on the theme of *Reworlding: The Art of Living Systems.*

> From its inception, the project was intended to get people to explore the question "How do we think like a living planet?" In the past, I would have collected and created a series of articles and films, made them available for the participants, and created presentations to explore their ideas. Essentially, I would have planted proverbial seeds with the hope that the teams would discover their own path through the material. Intentionally or not, I likely would have defaulted to a knowledge transfer approach.
>
> Having been exposed to the idea of regenerative content creation, I began asking myself, "What's the developmental journey we can provoke and deepen within the context of this project?" Instead of just creating media to relate histories, concepts, and information, we're committing ourselves to the individual and collective development of participants. This has presented an opportunity not only to build the mind of the collective artists, but also to examine the core process, purpose, and value of our own studio.
>
> For instance, in addition to illuminating systemic effects, our core process also includes illuminating their systemic causes. Similarly, beyond the core purpose, to *discern truth*, we are cultivating the capacity to *discern multiple perspectives* on complex topics. And finally, our core value is to *demonstrate the potential efficacy of agency.* This is not just to make hope possible, but to empirically demonstrate the reality of what is possible.
>
> By examining the limits of the knowledge transfer approach, I've also shifted my role from thematic expert to resource, recognizing that my role and approach need to be designed from a higher-level perspective. This process has offered me a way to more closely examine my approach to presentational media. I've tended to work at the basic level of telling—communicating information in the role of expert—but my real aspiration is to create experiences in service of developmental processes. My

challenge has been to integrate media into these developmental processes effectively and in ways that catalyze new, creative thinking, rather than encourage the endless rehearsal of old thoughts. I'm still working on how to carry out this role, looking for new ways to explore key principles within stories, metaphors, and experiences.

Going Forward: Journal Entries

Emma Morris

Being able to distinguish among the paradigms has provided incredible clarity for me, and I can see the benefits it will bring to society in general. What surprised me most is how deeply ingrained the old paradigms are. The Levels of Paradigm Framework enables us to check whether, with the best intentions, we are getting stuck thinking in old ways, even while we're promoting new ones.

Dan Palmer

I feel that I've made an irreversible shift in my approach to podcast recordings in the future. I can consciously use them as opportunities to move beyond just sharing good information to developing discernment within myself, my guests, and the listening audience. It's lifting my work from doing good toward regenerating life.

David McConville

The regenerative life frameworks have helped me use a real-world project to explore how our studio's media productions can be improved by designing them to serve an ongoing developmental process. They've also reminded me of how difficult it is to focus and commit to my own developmental work. I generally do not journal, so it has been challenging to dedicate time to regular reflection on these questions. But it has been rewarding to see my thought processes unfold and evolve, and I'm inspired by the fact that the themes, value, purpose, and process of our various projects appear consistent and aligned. Clarity continues to emerge!

Additional Insight: Journal Entry

Sam Ford, whom we met in chapter 7, is director of cultural intelligence for Tiller Press at Simon & Schuster, a CBS company, and he is an affiliate of MIT's Program in Comparative Media Studies/Writing. He divides his time between Bowling Green, Kentucky, and New York City, where he is also a Knight News Innovation Fellow at Columbia University's Tow Center for Digital Journalism.

> With regard to the regenerative media content creator, there is an interesting dialogue going on about the concept of solutions journalism. The idea is that it's not enough to tell people what's wrong and give them two sides of the story. People, if they haven't been reduced to total apathy and despair, are inevitably going to want to know, "What's being done to fix it? Who are the people that are already working on solutions? What are those solutions, and are there ways that I can get involved and help?"
>
> But this isn't any part of how most people are taught to be journalists. Their view of the role is to write about what has happened today in the world, period. No time to think about the larger context and what is being done to address the harm that has been identified. This creates what I call the "over your morning coffee read about the plight of people who are worse off than you so that you can feel like you have done your penitence before you go on with the day."
>
> I know of a guy who had quit reading the news entirely for the past year. His friends would ask him, "Don't you feel like you're not doing your part?"
>
> He answered, "Well, I realized I wasn't doing anything to help with these issues that I was reading about anyway, so I decided that, if I'm not going to help, I'm just going to quit reading about them."
>
> I thought this was a good point. What good does it do for people to watch three minutes about some crisis on the evening broadcast? Does it help the plight of those who are suffering? No. Does it make us feel more connected to the world? Well, maybe, but what good does that do?
>
> I think it's an interesting and provocative question to ask what the purpose of mainstream content creation really is. What are we trying to do to change the world? What is our purpose beyond making money or

making audiences more cosmopolitan, more knowledgeable about the plights of other people? I agree that we should care about what is happening elsewhere. But how do we take any kind of action in response, and how often are those actions, when they do occur, anything more than superficial stabs at fixing problems?

I think a lot of journalists are struggling to come to terms with the fact that they got into the field in order to create a more informed and engaged citizenry, to be a pillar of democracy. It's painful to hear citizens report that "reading your content makes me feel hopeless, makes me want to disengage from the world." It's the opposite of the benefit they thought they were providing. So the content creator essence triad makes perfect sense to me. It shows the orders of commitment and effect a media person should be aiming for, and by implication it points out how often we fall short.

CHAPTER TWELVE

The Regenerative Spirit Resource Role

WITHOUT A SIGNIFICANT AMOUNT of work and training, human beings have a nearly universal tendency to fall into repetitive patterns of thought and behavior. At a minimum, these patterns contribute to the feeling that we're in a rut, a comfortable prison. At their worst, they lead to feelings of meaninglessness, despair, and even suicide. Either way, we become risk averse and dare not disturb the threadbare familiarity of our own habits.

Sometimes we feel an inner prompting to break out of prison, to change our lives and strike out into unknown territory. More often we are shocked out of our complacency by a dramatic event: a death, the loss of a job, a natural disaster, or the end of a primary relationship. If we are lucky, this is the juncture where we reach out to or find ourselves taken in hand by a spirit resource.

Because habitualization and loss of way are universal human phenomena, the spirit resource role is also universal, present in every culture at every time. It is played formally by priests, ministers, shamans, or psychotherapists. It can be played informally by a wise aunt, mentor, coach, or friend. In each case, the spirit resource seeks to dislodge us from stuck patterns and reconnect us to higher and more-encompassing perspectives. One of the reasons we are willing to seek assistance and disruption from such people, even when we refuse to accept advice from others closer to us, is that we perceive them to be neutral but caring, unattached to any outcome other than our own awakening.

You might say that this book and the research behind it are themselves examples of spirit resourcing. By disrupting conventional ideas about the meaning and purpose of the nine roles explored here, the regenerative life research project had the effect of bringing new spirit, perspective, and energy to participants. Rather than telling them what to do, it gave them frameworks from which to invent new ways to carry out their lifework, and it resourced their efforts along the way.

Like the regenerative educator role, the spirit resource role frequently shows up in the work of each of the other roles. When any of us engage regeneratively with our families, friends, colleagues, and clients, we lift them to a higher level, and although this can be destabilizing at first, in the end it is almost always experienced as revitalizing and renewing. However, a caution: it is *extremely important* to gain people's permission (implicitly or explicitly) before working with them in this deep and intimate way. Otherwise, we risk showing up as a trickster, jester, or clown—effective but also brutal; these are venerable roles in almost all traditions, but they are no longer recognized as acceptable in most social and cultural contexts.

The Essence of the Regenerative Spirit Resource

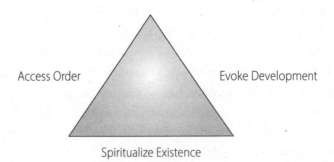

Access Order

Evoke Development

Spiritualize Existence

The regenerative spirit resource's core process is to *evoke development*. Development is a lifelong process. It moves us through different phases as we mature in terms of managing higher levels of complexity, unpredictability, and conflict, and as we rise to increasingly challenging tasks. We often fall back to earlier developmental phases, especially in times of stress. The work of the spirit resource is to use questions and reflection as instruments to assess where we are developmentally and to help us regain our aspiration to move forward.

The role's core purpose is to *spiritualize existence*. A spirit resource helps remind us that our existence, no matter how bleak or joyful it may appear, is not limited to our current situation. There is always a larger world of potential, meaning, and connectedness within and around us, and only our repetitive personal stories make us blind to it. The spirit resource reminds us to connect to the heart or essence of ourselves and others, our relationships, and our actions. This connection forms a doorway by which our spirits can be lifted and our world regenerated.

The spirit resource's core value is to *access order*. The word *order* has a specific meaning in regenerative contexts (as illustrated in chapter 1 by the story of our soccer player). It refers to a shift in level of system or perception. As we move up in order, the complexity and potential of the system we're looking at shifts accordingly, and thus a shift in order can radically alter our perspective.

When we think about a question from our own perspective versus seeing it from the perspective of family, community, or society, we feel a contraction or shutting down, a kind of darkening. For example, to a person hopelessly locked into polarized conflict with a life partner, it may appear that all ease and happiness has been sucked from the world. What an enormous relief it is to discover a third, higher-order way of seeing that reconciles the values of both partners, understanding them as mutual and complementary contributors to a shared purpose. A regenerative spirit resource seeks to build this capability for ordering and the shifts in perspective it enables, so that it can be accessed whenever a person needs it.

Experiencing the Regenerative Spirit Resource Role

Samia Abou-Samra lives in Brooklyn, New York, and is the cofounder and CEO of Turtle Tank, which he describes as a "modern-day mystery school, where we ignite radical purpose, support the evolution of consciousness, and harness creative power to bring forth worlds of radical love and freedom." Reflecting on his participation in the research project, he wrote,

> Recently our team has evolved Turtle Tank from an Incubator for Radical Entrepreneurs to an Incubator for Radical Love and Freedom. The basic premise has changed from helping people start and grow their enterprises to igniting purpose to create new worlds. The regenerative life project has given me language to describe this change as a shift from doing good to regenerating. Though we had already been focused on regeneration in many ways, our message, vision, and container didn't clearly reflect this orientation. Yet this is precisely why our work stood out in the first place, why our community stuck around. We *evoke development*. Our community members would jokingly say that we "tricked" them into thinking they were working on their enterprises, when in reality, they were healing and being revitalized as more purposeful and powerful human beings.
>
> I know that my success is due to a foundational commitment to realigning with and deepening into essence and purpose. This is resonant with the idea of *spiritualizing existence*. The community that works with us at Turtle Tank has witnessed a steady organic growth, development, and deepening of our work through significant shifts. These were not simply changes in direction based on feedback. They resulted from reinvestigation and realignment with our internal core purpose, process, and value—efforts I find especially necessary during the first few years in the development of any project. The more easily we surrender to the practice of respiritualizing existence, the more magnetic and impactful our work and project become.
>
> A key thing I've learned from the research project is that I play the role of regenerative spirit resource throughout my life. This seems simple, but it is deeply profound and life changing for me. For years I have been resisting my full alignment with this role. In fact, I believe that our

current dominant culture is so influenced by the Value Return Paradigm that it has diminished the importance of resourcing spirit. As a result, we have become divorced from the sacred, from spirit, from accepting the unique essence and purpose of each and every element on Earth.

As I understand the regenerative life frameworks, the spirit resource is actually core to the entire system. Spirit resources are responsible for igniting, evoking, or enabling our reason for existing and helping us to *access higher orders* of understanding. Without this, our lives are meaningless, whatever roles we play. Our understanding of our essence and purpose is at the foundation of the evolutionary process. Our very survival depends on this understanding. Spirit drives our evolution and continued existence as a species. Without it at the core, we can neither create nor sustain a regenerative culture.

Finding the Right Level

Rei Chou lives in Los Angeles, California, and is the founder of The Feast, a global initiative that works to bring about change by inviting people to share dinner. It's a simple idea that has brought thousands of people together in communities around the world. She explains,

> I applied what I was learning about the regenerative spirit resource to a friend and collaborator who had come over to ask me for personal support. In the past, I probably would have approached this interaction from the levels of value return and arrest disorder. I would have tried to understand his issues with respect to his relationships so that I could use my intuitive and energy work to help. I would also have considered how his issues relate to our potential for collaboration and what that relationship might be. While this consideration would ultimately have been for our mutual gain, it was clearly originating at the value return level.
>
> After my exposure to the role of spirit resource, I began to recognize a higher-level purpose for my relationships and interactions with others. I was in these conversations for a *reason*—to help people connect with themselves and their essences, but also to connect them with something larger. Our conversations were happening within a systemic

context, which meant that spirit was engaging *through* me. My interactions weren't just for the benefit of a singular me or them; my purpose was to unlock greater potential for whole systems of people.

With regard to engaging my friend, I resolved to hold a bigger picture, including considering how I could serve the community through my relationship with him. My intention to support the whole in connection with spirit lifted our conversation up to the regenerate level. My focus shifted from applying my gifts to help him to cultivating a sense of connection that would support the composition of the entire community he was creating.

The result was a deepening of our relationship and a path of engagement and support, opening possibilities for collaboration that would have been invisible to me from a value exchange point of view. Instead of healing this person, I've stepped into a co-created process that will develop us both.

Applying the Seven First Principles

Curtis Ogden lives in Amherst, Massachusetts, where he is a senior associate of the Boston-based Interaction Institute for Social Change. The institute builds collaborative capacity in individuals, communities, organizations, and networks that are working for social justice and environmental sustainability. At the time of the regenerative life research project, Curtis was working on a second Network Leadership Lab for self-selected staff members of a global conservation organization, part of an effort to create a paradigm shift within the field of conservation. Here are some of his journal reflections:

> My participation in the research project, along with my ongoing internal work over the course of the past year, has helped me interrupt my typical, heroic do-good patterns. Working in the second lab with some of the same people I'd worked with earlier, in a first lab, gave me a chance to compare my approaches before and after learning about the regenerative spirit resource role.
>
> For the second lab, my partners and I engaged in an emergent process for designing and delivering the lab experience. We were clear

that the second lab couldn't be a replication of the first, in spite of its success and the enthusiastic response we had gotten. We wanted to go deeper, and that could not be fully planned ahead. We needed to be in flow, in the moment, continuously asking what life was asking of us. We needed to get to know the new *whole* in the room: the group and the systems that they were focused on. We needed to see ourselves grounded in the *essence* of that whole, neither separate from nor at the center of it. And we needed to create space for a self-directing impulse to take hold, without forcing it.

By the second day, I found myself tuning in more deeply and following the underlying energy in the room. This enabled me to hold the whole and freed my co-leaders to work with individual participants. It also opened up space for a few spontaneous actions, including one in which the group self-organized to address an injustice and terrible strategic lapse that had been identified within the broader organization and that was impacting one of the people in the room. This action has already borne fruit, a manifestation of *potential* in the group that had not until that moment found expression. It also led to a very moving, and again self-organized, closing circle, within which a number of people expressed a profound sense of belonging.

I am still heartened and a bit stunned by the effort that has ensued since the end of the workshop. For me, it points to a natural inclination toward *development* in the direction of more regenerative ways of being. A move toward life! It has also led to conversations with others about the need for a paradigm shift within the broader organization. I am continuing to check in with some of the lab participants around what this might look like, even as they do things differently in their own networks. In the process, I feel myself becoming a more powerful resource to the collective spirit of the group, which in turn feeds me.

Managing Inner Obstacles

Ana Gabriela Robles is an entrepreneur, corporate responsibility consultant, and ceremonial leader. She lives in Mexico City, and her work takes her to many other parts of Latin America. She recently used the regenerative life frameworks to upgrade a ceremony she offers, called "The Red

Tent," which is designed to empower women to take charge of their own bodies and health.

During the ceremony, I became distracted by a woman who kept interrupting to ask questions about what we were doing. Each time, she wrote down my answer and, before long, interrupted again with a new question. I noticed myself getting paranoid, *fabricating* stories about why she wanted to pull all of this information out of me. It felt as if I was being value extracted! I was also becoming angry and frustrated, afraid that we were drifting away from our purpose for the ceremony and that I wouldn't be able both to fill her needs and meet the expectations of the group.

I paused and grounded myself in the spirit resource essence. I was here to evoke her development and to spiritualize existence for her and the whole group. When I gave myself this little space, it became obvious to me that she had the least background experience of anyone in the ceremony. She was trying to fill the gap with information, when what she really needed was experience. I explained this to her and offered to be a guide into the experiences she was seeking, rather than a recipe book filled with answers to her questions. Immediately the tension in the group was broken. She continued making notes, but she stopped asking so many questions. And the group as a whole stepped in to support her, sharing stories of their own experiences of women's medicine and sacred ritual space.

The outcome was a very happy person who understands fully what it means to be a Red Tent Guardian! She gave us all a gift by helping us to become conscious that this work is not only about knowledge in the mind but also about state of being. Everyone in the workshop came to understand how important it is to have a deep inner experience of the material before they try to share it with other circles.

Generating a New Pattern

Trevanna Grenfell, who lives in Unity, Maine, is founder and director of the Wildwood Path. She describes her spirit guide role as work at "the intersection of wilderness skills and strategic consulting." She aims to "integrate practical outdoor skills and ecosystem thinking into individual and team leadership development in order to leverage deep nature connection as an avenue for social change."

In her journal, Trevanna describes how she and a client group lifted the design of a new program from the do-good level to the regenerative level.

Recently I was hired by a large botanic garden to assist their staff with the design of a program to support teens through transformative coming-of-age experiences in nature. This was a complex assignment that involved working both experientially, through edgy outdoor programming, and theoretically, through reflective strategizing sessions. I worked with the teens themselves, as well as with the environmental education staff and the executive director of the gardens. Ostensibly I was there to impart tools, but I soon realized that my primary role would be to facilitate all of the participants' connections with the natural world and their own best selves. My aim was to foster the inspiration and transcendence that is the hallmark of a true connection with the mysterious force we call *spirit*.

In the past, I would have focused primarily on the information, experiences, and skills I could have conveyed to the team of staff members. I would have assumed that if the staff and teens knew the mentoring models, curriculum design strategies, and specific activities I employed, then they would be able to enact a meaningful program and there would be a positive impact. This might have been true, but we would have missed out totally on what happened when I changed my thinking about the role I was playing and approached it more regeneratively.

I focused on how to bring forth the teams' own unique sources of inspiration, motivation, and skillful facilitation, including memories, relationships with the land, and collaborations with one another and other partners. In practice, this occurred through a mix of deep listening and reflecting on the ways in which they were already working at the regenerate life level. I disrupted assumptions about the roles of humans versus nature or teachers versus students and offered questions and experiences that helped them clarify their own thinking and their reasons for doing the work.

By establishing in advance the goal to facilitate connection, I kept myself anchored to an uplifted aim, rather than just to the transference of information. I was able to keep this aim in mind and let it inform my thinking and the ways I listened and asked questions. In the end, I did share some information and activities with the team, but only in response to their genuine requests and openness to receiving new tools.

Over the course of two days, I saw inspiration, connection, and new realization light up their eyes. I heard them speak with increasing clarity and enthusiasm about their own aims and skills when it came to facilitating connection for others. At the close, they developed a shared vision for an interwoven series of programs that included families, youth of all ages, and support for and from elders. They also identified a slowly growing set of leadership capabilities that would enable them to offer deeply transformative, nature-based coming-of-age programs for teens.

With this big and beautiful vision guiding them, they were motivated and excited to get started. One of them said at the end, "At first I saw this as just another program that we could offer. Now I realize that it's an opportunity to do things really differently. I can see that I have a lot more to learn about moving toward these deep experiences of transformation and reciprocity with nature."

By focusing on lifting up the essence of each person, along with the essence of the unique project the group was envisioning, I was able to support them in a profound and developmental way. This enabled them to design a nature program that was uniquely relevant to their group and their place.

Going Forward: Journal Entries

Samia Abou-Samra

I'm less and less invested in the Do Good Paradigm because it encourages us to unconsciously impose our definition of good on others. This is just another form of control. I'm invested in awakening regenerative lives and, in my own life, expressing essence as a form of inspiration for others. I want to provide the framework and ecosystem for this resourcing.

Rei Chou

I'm often in exploratory conversations with individuals, organizations, and movements about all sorts of possibilities. I want to engage them in this inquiry, asking, "What is the whole that I'm serving? That we're serving?" When I don't come from a self-focused or even other-focused perspective but consider instead the largest level of possibility for all who might be affected, I begin to know where and how I can have the highest impact. I also hope to understand myself better as I learn where my service is most effective.

The value of this work is to help give people a sense of their *why*. In a world where people are looking for purpose, the regenerative life roles offer structure that supports meaningful work. They also enable interactions that clarify without being reductive and constricting. I believe that when we see ourselves as part of and in service to larger systems, we have a greater sense of our own power to affect those systems. We ground our self-worth in our potential impact on the world and our sense of connection to the whole.

Curtis Ogden

I see myself continuing to ask the question "What is the living whole here, and what does it need?" Such a powerful and vitalizing way to redirect attention! I am excited to see the trust that can grow and the energy that can be channeled from taking this approach—for me, those I serve, and the systems in which we participate. I also think that mindfulness of inner obstacles is key, helping me gain greater self-mastery in service to the regenerative future I so want for all of us.

Ana Gabriela Robles

Engaging in this role from an essence perspective allows me to exit the coach or therapist mode and focuses me on resourcing from the spirit aspect of life, helping individuals and groups find their developmental paths. Going forward I want to explore all of the regenerative life roles, to internalize their essence triads and become conscious of when and how they come into play. I also want to be able to discern when to pull from one or the other to uplift any given situation.

Trevanna Grenfell

By consciously inhabiting my role as spirit resource, I can support my consulting and mentoring clients as they unearth and act from their own essences and deep connections with nature. This will create conditions for them to step into their own capacities much more easily than if I just offered my own ideas. Moving forward, I see myself continuing to hone my ability to get my ego out of the way so that I can truly be a resource. This approach has a ripple effect that inspires and motivates me to keep growing and working for societal transformation.

Additional Insight: Journal Entries

Carmen von Luckwald, another project participant, lives in Copenhagen, Denmark, where she is self-employed as a ceremonial leader. She applied what she learned from the regenerative life research project to a recent cacao ceremony for women.

> The aim I set as I approached this ceremony was to demand more of the work I do and bring everyone to a higher level of understanding. Ceremonies and spiritual contexts in our current culture often end up as nothing more than a break from everyday life. I wanted to go beyond this, helping us collectively take a first step toward regenerating our lives in all aspects.
>
> I opened in a way that was intended from the beginning to elevate the mind-set and expectations of everyone involved. I explained my main principles and the understanding that underlies my work. I referred explicitly to my role as *resource*, conveying the belief that there is no external expert who knows better than we do. "You all already hold the knowledge of what you need and how you can regenerate your life and energy. I will create a space to allow you to return to that source of knowledge and energy so that you can come to know and remember it."
>
> When I look back at the ceremony, I can see that I learned some important things. I had higher expectations of myself and what we could achieve collectively, and thus I was able to invite everyone up the ladder to a different level. Also, I realized that in spiritual work, we need to communicate clearly that we are not service providers, as this is what our culture has been teaching us lately. It really helped to see myself as a resource to the work of others. It also helped to have a framework in

mind that I could share with participants. This enabled me to create a less-structured ceremony, while still holding a very clear direction.

Kerstin Graebner lives in Chennai, India. She is the founder and managing director of Parinama Inspired Living, whose stated purpose is "empowering individuals to rediscover and reestablish harmony in their inner worlds, with other human beings, and with nature." Here are some of her reflections:

One part of me sees listening as a major aspect of spirit resourcing. In a world where we talk at each other rather than with each other, I believe that something new can emerge from being listened to. This is where my work adds real value. I have seen many times that being listened to is not only healing (arresting disorder), it also initiates a process for the one who has been listened to, awakening a desire to contribute to others and the world in return, and to be who we really are (regeneration).

However, I can also use my listening skills as a default, a way of avoiding confrontation. I recently found myself in a negotiation where I was stuck in the Value Return Paradigm, unable to hold a regenerative view. I came out of the conversation feeling a sense of regret for not having used the opportunity to express myself clearly and fully. There was some shame around seeing an old pattern play out again. When I journaled about it, I realized that the conversation was not complete for me.

The next day, I followed up the first conversation with a very open and honest dialogue, in which I remained more connected to myself and the intention to come from a regenerative perspective. The two of us decided not to work together right now, but we committed to staying in touch in order to collaborate when we are both clearer about what we want to accomplish together.

This was very different from what I usually consider a good outcome. I normally prefer to go forward with collaboration, regardless of my energy and inspiration, trusting that spirit will flow once we enter the doing. However, the true opportunity that the regenerative perspective revealed was to step back from the Value Return Paradigm. This will allow us to regroup and return to the conversation when we are both aligned with who we are and who we want to be. Only then, I am convinced, can we offer a genuinely transformational experience for those who work with us and support them as they bring forth their own essences.

If more people had access to this material, we'd be living in a different world. It gives me immense hope to have had a chance to try it out for myself and continue to engage with it in the future. On first encounter, what surprised me most was how baffled my mind was, how overwhelmed by trying to grasp the frameworks, how challenging it felt to disentangle the layers of my own experience. This approach is complex, in the best and most challenging of ways, as complex as life. That's what inspires me—the opportunity to sit with the complexity, to see what it does to me, and to be with the confusion and the emerging clarity, alike.

To me, this is aliveness, learning, and growth. I am sure that in our lifetimes we will see the Regenerate Life Paradigm get grounded more and more in our communities and families. We will all have to develop the capacity to hold the complexity and the not-knowing and the in-between as we move away from the old ways to the even older regenerative ways that we have forgotten. I am committed to stretching into the essence of this role as much as I possibly can. That, to me, means making the best possible use of my life.

Conclusion: Nodal Roles for a Regenerative Society

ALWAYS START WORK, personal and professional, with a framework. It's a deeply engrained practice that helps me improve the discipline and wholeness of my thinking. So when I sat down to outline this book and design the regenerative life research project, I knew that I needed to discover an underlying structure to give them systemic coherence. The process took a little while. I started with a simpler, five-term system (the pentad), but it just didn't encompass the kind of major social transformation that I was trying to conceptualize. I kept adding terms, building more and more complex ways of looking at the subject. When I got to nine terms, it all snapped into focus.

The classic depiction of a nine-term system is the enneagram, an ancient mathematical instrument and esoteric symbol, which in some traditions is traced to early Zoroastrian thought. In recent decades it has been widely adopted as a way to describe personality types. Unfortunately, this contradicts its use as a framework to understand dynamic forces at play in the transformation of living systems. By mapping the regenerative roles onto an enneagram, my intention is to depict the integrated work required to transform whole societies. In its original iteration, the enneagram I generated described nine foundational arenas of work that act together to sustain a healthy society. These served as the basis for defining the nine regenerative roles.

The Work of Sustaining a Healthy Society

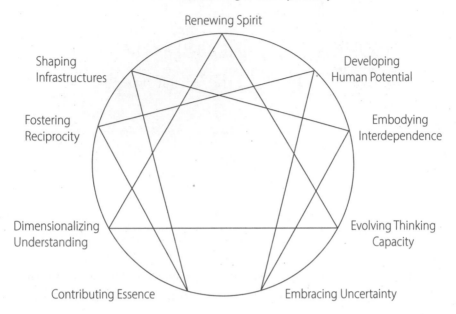

Developing human potential is necessary because we are born as unfinished beings. The good life could be defined as one in which we discover and learn how to express our potential. Helping establish children on this path is one of a *parent's* critical tasks (whether this is a biological or an extended family sort of parent). Without it, a society becomes greatly diminished.

Embracing uncertainty is the way free people engage creatively with the opportunities and hazards that life inevitably presents. *Design* is the means by which they utilize uncertainty to discover and express the potential that lies within them and the situations they encounter.

Embodying interdependence is the means by which humans secure their place within the planetary web of life. Through the power of their technologies, modern societies have fostered the illusion that humans can live in a bubble, disconnected from all of the natural forces that govern life on Earth. *Earth tenders* remind us that our health as individuals and societies depends on remembering our place within living systems.

Shaping infrastructures is the activity that enables people to create the governing and operating systems that will materialize their collective agreements. All of these infrastructures can be built and rebuilt, although some, such as national constitutions, have been designed to slow down the rebuilding process. Whether an infrastructure supports national governance or local trash collection, it belongs to *citizens*, who are ultimately responsible for how it is shaped.

Contributing essence is what free societies should encourage if they are to remain vital and innovative. Social conventions can all too easily favor conformity over the unpredictability and variety of human uniqueness and creative contribution. When this happens, the *entrepreneurial* spirit that always looks for ways to make things better can be lost or thwarted. A truly pluralistic society, one that is oriented to potential, values the entrepreneurialism to be found in everyone.

Fostering reciprocity is the means by which enduring and equitable economies are created. One of the reasons that extreme wealth inequality is so destructive is that people at both the top and the bottom of the system lose their ability to see a connection with the common good. Reciprocity is grounded in the idea that our contributions are essential to the health and evolution of whole systems, and that with them, our own sustenance can be ensured. Making this possible is the essential work of the *economic shaper*.

Evolving thinking capacity is work that we must learn to do if we are to become capable of playing any of the other key roles. Too much of what passes for thinking is actually rehashing old thoughts rather than creating new ones. For this reason, an *educator* pushes people to move beyond information consumption or borrowing other people's thoughts to active generation of their own thoughts and intelligent management of their own thinking processes.

Dimensionalizing understanding is the special work of the *media content creator*, who stimulates and supports us in our unending quests to see more profoundly into what is true. By challenging us to enlarge, deepen, broaden, disrupt, complexify, diversify, contest, and interpret, the media creator invites us to engage all of our mental capacities to grow an understanding of the world that will allow us to make wise choices.

Renewing spirit is necessary if a society is to come together to address the challenges presented by an ever-changing world. A community or nation or even a soccer team that has become dispirited loses the will to gather itself and try again. I call the person who fulfills this vital role *spirit resource*. Nearly all of us are called upon to play this role from time to time for our friends, families, the groups that we lead, or the nations to which we belong, when they have lost hope and need to be reminded of the meaning and significance of their lives or their efforts.

Used to as a dynamic framework, the enneagram has traditionally guided change by identifying the key energies or arenas that must be present for a system to gain the capacity to transform or evolve itself. Each of the nine roles on our enneagram provides a conceptual container that individuals can use to invent their own contributions to the work of transforming society.

I said at the beginning that the work is non-heroic. It's not about quitting our jobs and manning the barricades. It's about finding better, more enlivening ways to think about and play the roles that we have chosen. In other words, it comes back to Mahatma Gandhi's observation that inner change is the most effective way to manifest the outer change we want to see in the world.

Epilogue: Take It Personally.
Take It to Work.

Dear Reader:

I hope that you will do something with what you have read in these pages. If you've gotten this far, chances are that this is exactly what you intend. For your project to continue living a regenerative life, I have three suggestions.

Notice the Differences

You might have sensed that what I've presented here is quite different from conventional training or self-help approaches. This is true, and I'd like to make some of these differences explicit, which can perhaps be done best by expressing them as principles.

Lead from essence, not from personality.

This applies to us as individuals; we make our most distinctive contributions when we remain true to ourselves. This also applies to how we approach all the people, places, and materials around us that make up our experience of the world. When we engage them from their essences, rather than from their superficial characteristics or from the abstract ideas we form about them, we stand the greatest chance of treating them with respect and drawing from them their full potential.

To live this way, we may need to break a very common habit, which is the tendency to lump things (including ourselves) into categories. In case I haven't made it perfectly clear, I will restate here that you are *not* one of the nine roles laid out in *The Regenerative Life*. As a human being, you have the potential to step into and out of most, if not all, of these roles, but not one of them will ever become what you are. That would substitute a temporary pattern of working for your own unique essence, the root of who you really are.

And I caution you that this applies to all typologies, including others that use the enneagram as an organizing structure. Any way of understanding individuals by sorting them into categories oversimplifies the complexities and emerging possibilities of a unique human life by reducing it to a broadly general pattern of behaviors or tendencies.

Move from a static to a dynamic view of life.

Because we humans are all works in progress, we can continue to grow and evolve throughout our lives, but to do so requires a certain kind of mental discipline. We must challenge the many fixed beliefs we hold about who and how we are. We often lose sight of our own capacity for change, just as we write off other people, believing that they can't or won't change. This does them, and us, a disservice.

The trick is to find ways to observe and consciously participate in changes that occur within us. This means looking beyond our current patterns or habits to watch the evolution in our thoughts, actions, effects, and outcomes. Instead of asking who you are being now, ask what you see yourself becoming. Here are some questions that can shift you to a more dynamic outlook: *What is changing in my thinking, actions, effects, and outcomes? How are they different than they were yesterday? What can evolve next, if I direct effort to it? What is my aim in this regard? What will I choose to observe as the change unfolds?*

Use regenerative frameworks, not models, to guide thinking.

Models are useful when the aim is to produce replicability, standardization, and easy measurement. They are prescriptive and definitive, offering predictable answers about how things work or should work. A classic example is, "Ready, aim, fire!"

But models can help us make decisions about the world only as we currently know it. They are not capable of producing singularity and transformation, within which the essence of something can shine and be evolved. That is the work of regenerative frameworks, which reveal the dynamics of living systems, including the relationships and arenas that inform them and the potential toward which they could evolve. Frameworks don't provide answers; they offer ways to pursue open discovery. Think, for example, of the Levels of Paradigm Framework and the kind of ongoing inquiry that it invites. Models promote knowledge; they cannot lead us to the understanding that this kind of framework enables.

Journal Developmentally

Journaling provided a core practice for those who participated in the regenerative life action research, and it provided the material from which this book was drawn. Written reflection was undertaken in a very specific and developmental way. Instead of simply asking participants to describe what they were doing, I introduced regenerative concepts and frameworks for the purpose of shaking up their existing assumptions and thought patterns. Journaling gave them an opportunity to notice and reflect on the internal shifts that began to occur as a result. In other words, the project was designed to use journaling as a way to grow participants' consciousness of who they were choosing to become.

I encourage you to create a journal for yourself as you explore new ways to play your roles in society, and I've developed a simple framework to help you in this effort. I've named it with the acronym, FORM. It captures four aspects of developmental work that journaling can support.

- **F**ramework thinking
- **O**bserving obstacles
- **R**eframing/reordering
- **M**astering self

I chose these activities because they evoke and affirm our active role in self-creation and the proactive reflection that journaling is intended to stimulate. I've used the word *mastering* instead of mastery, as a reminder that the process is open-ended and always evolving.

I also offer a process to follow as you prepare for and then reflect on a given day or event. It can be applied to any of the regenerative roles that you undertake, but remember to keep it concrete by linking it to what you have chosen to work on within a specific context. It is always tempting to make generalizations about ourselves and our lives, but opportunities for the creation of breakthroughs only ever arise in real activities and events.

1. *Framework thinking:* What framework will I use to examine or design a development approach to this day or event? For example, how can the Seven First Principles of Regeneration help me generate a more complete picture of what I'm working on, and what can they tell me about an evolutionary path I could pursue?

2. *Observing obstacles:* With regard to this day or event, which of the inner obstacles do I see at work as I pursue my objectives and goals? Can I see what triggers them? How is my ability to be self-managing evolving in this regard? What pattern changes do I see? Where do I see opportunities to engage further?

3. *Reframing/reordering:* With regard to this day or event, what paradigm did I engage from? How do I want to evolve my ability to consciously activate and engage a higher paradigm?

4. *Mastering self:* With regard to this day or event, what is the new pattern that I seek to move toward? How can I state this as an aim for myself, a new state of being that I wish to stretch and grow into? *Over time:* What is evolving in me? In my aim?

Note also that FORM is a set of four mantras, very short phrases to remember and reference throughout the day, as a way to remind yourself of ways to lift your work to the regenerative level and to reflect as you go.

Join a Regenerative Community

Joining a regenerative community significantly increases the joy and rewards of regenerative living. Currently, a large and growing community is forming around the ideas in *The Regenerative Life*. You can access more information by visiting the websites listed below, listening to the podcasts that are available, or joining one of the online communities that work with these materials in an ongoing way. All of these resources and more can be accessed at theregenerativelife.org/communities.

Communities

- *The Regenerative Life Communities*
  - The Regenerative Women-Entrepreneur Community
    A Fusion of live and online events, helping to increase wisdom and collaboration among women leaders in both the for-profit and nonprofit worlds
  - The Regenerative Parenting Community
    Live online events (and some local events), applying principles of the Regenerate Life Paradigm to being a parent—also relevant for grandparents, adopted parents, stepparents, foster parents, and others who play a major role in the lives of children.
  - More to come. Subscribe to our e-newsletter to stay up to date!

- *The Regenerative Business Communities.* Business teams working together in live online workshops to learn to build non-displaceable, disruptive innovation, in their own businesses and industries and in social and planetary imperatives. The workshop series flows from Strategy to Leadership to Management/Work Design. Ten to fifteen companies working together with Carol Sanford and the Regenerative Business Alliance.

- *Change Agent Development Communities.* Live in many communities in the United States. Fusion (local and live online) around the world.

  Learn to work with others as a resource.

Podcasts and Blogs

- *Business Second Opinion.* Critiquing *Harvard Business Review* articles, one idea at a time.
- *The Regenerative Business.* Interviews with business leaders in pursuit of a regenerative business.
- *The Responsible Capitalist.* Interviewing economic shapers who are promoting the regenerative life with ideas, endeavors, and money.
- *The Regenerative Life Podcast.* Interviews and stories of people pursuing the processes described in *The Regenerative Life* and more.

In Closing

Think of yourself as unfinished, a living expression of your own potential. Don't get stuck in pigeonholes of your own or others' making. You are not a number. You are not a type. Nor are you an average, a statistic, or a demographic, in spite of all the ways the world tries to categorize you as one or all of the above.

You are a unique being in a living world filled with other unique beings, and we all rely on you to play your part. Your lifelong task is to grow, deepen, and evolve yourself as a member of this living world so that its liveliness and continual regeneration become manifest in you, your actions, and what you create. This is central to what it means to work from the Regenerate Life Paradigm.

Thank you for joining us in this hopeful, caring work.

Take risks!

Carol Sanford

Notes

Introduction: We Need a Better Theory

1. John Heider, *The Tao of Leadership: Lao Tzu's* Tao Te Ching *Adapted for a New Age* (Atlanta: Humanics Publishing Group, 1997).
2. Sarita Chawla and John Renesch, eds., *Learning Organizations: Developing Cultures for Tomorrow's Workplace* (New York: Productivity Press, 1995).

Chapter One: Beyond the Heroic

1. Edwin Abbott, *Flatland: A Romance of Many Dimensions*, rev. ed. (1884), https://www.gutenberg.org/files/201/201-h/201-h.htm.
2. For more on this, see "Three Criteria for Growing Human Capacity," in chapter 3 of Carol Sanford's *The Regenerative Business: Redesign Work, Cultivate Human Potential, Achieve Extraordinary Outcomes* (Boston: Nicholas Brealey Publishing, 2017).
3. David Bohm, *Thought as a System* (New York: Routledge, 1994).

Chapter Six: The Regenerative Earth Tender Role

1. M. Kat Anderson, *Tending the Wild: Native American Knowledge and the Management of California's Natural Resources* (Berkeley, CA: University of California Press, 2013).

Index